THESE WERE THE HOURS

Memories of My Hours Press

Réanville and Paris

1928–1931

By

NANCY CUNARD

Edited with a Foreword by

Hugh Ford

Southern Illinois University Press

Carbondale and Edwardsville

Feffer & Simons

London and Amsterdam

For Bertram Rota and Walter Lowenfels,
friends of the Hours Press

Foreword

The network of tiny expatriate presses, founded on slim budgets by émigrés from England and the United States who migrated to France, usually Paris, in the twenties and thirties, all but collapsed shortly before the Second World War. But for nearly twenty years private presses like William Bird's Three Mountains, Harry and Caresse Crosby's Black Sun, and Robert McAlmon's Contact Editions superseded one another, bravely confronted (if never quite solved) the enigmas of publishing in a foreign country, survived incredible financial crises, and to their everlasting credit turned out impressive, well-designed books by Ezra Pound, Ernest Hemingway, William Carlos Williams, James Joyce, and among the lesser luminaries, Hart Crane, Kay Boyle, and Gertrude Stein.

Operating a press abroad was, to say the least, precarious, particularly if funds were short, which was nearly always the case. But fortunately, besides the usually elusive but occasionally real dividends, there were a few tangible compensations which publishers could expect. Since in most instances they were themselves authors, or hoped to be, they had created at least one marketplace, however small, for their own writing (and, as it turned out, for that of many of their friends as well), which more often than not had been rejected by a commercial publisher. Their presses did more than operate as welcome outlets for unwanted books, however; the fact of their existence symbolized the protest of a whole contingent of writers who opposed what they considered the overcommercialization of the established publishing houses. If exile presses could promise their authors only a small printing, say between one hundred and five hundred copies, and a decidedly limited circulation (which was what they generally did promise), authors at least felt they were being granted a hearing, which was more than they had ever had before. In addition, and of no negligible compensation for both authors and publishers, was the shared creativity involved in jointly preparing a book for publication. Although occasionally stormy, relations between writers and publishers generally developed into happy collaborations that were mutually creative and stimulating and resulted in publications that satisfied both. The truth of the foregoing statement finds an exciting documentation in the brief but happy life of the Hours Press and its ebullient owner, Nancy Cunard, who from 1928 to 1931 coaxed enough writing from established authors as well as literary fledglings to fill twenty-four books, a figure that far exceeds the output of any other private press for a comparable period.

Nancy Cunard's name and background are, of course, synonymous with power and wealth. The granddaughter of Samuel Cunard, founder of the ship company, and daughter of Sir Bache Cunard and Lady (Maud) Emerald, a socialite from San Francisco, she was born in 1896 in the Leicestershire country estate of Nevill Holt, which local legend proclaimed had been created originally as "a hunting-box for William Rufus." There Sir Bache had brought his American bride, and there amidst the panoply of Victorian finery collected and fastidiously arranged by her socially conscious mother, Nancy Cunard spent her childhood, alone, except for her ubiquitous governess, and a gentleman who often came to her parents' house for long periods: the gentleman was the Irish novelist, George Moore.

Moore's affection for Lady Cunard, though perhaps not as intense as the devotion Yeats showed for Maud Gonne, reached in the end the same impasse of love given but unreturned. But from the time of their first meeting in 1895 until 1910–11, when "another took first place in Lady Cunard's affections," George Moore's adoration for Emerald Cunard must at least have equalled that which Yeats bestowed upon his Irish Maud. And long afterwards, as his letters to her reveal, he continued to watch and worship her from a distance.

The sojourns of George Moore at Nevill Holt brought him (to young Nancy he was the man with "a bubbling hot dish of a voice") and the daughter of his beloved Emerald together often, so often that in recollecting this period in her memoir of G.M., as Moore was always known to his friends, Miss Cunard has called him "her first friend." The appellation could hardly be more accurate. When she was four, he twitted her on "advancing" from *Reading without Tears* to *The Violet Fairy Book*; at ten, he was delighted to learn that she had been secretly reading Elinor Glyn's "wicked" novel, *Three Weeks*; at fifteen, on their last walks through the countryside near Holt, he discussed with her "French painting and English poetry," and tried, none too successfully, to explain what it was he meant by "objective verse." Nonetheless, she was made a collaborator and joined in the search for "objective" poems to fill his anthology of *Pure Poetry*. Later, her accounts of school in Munich, where she studied music and German, Russian, and Scandinavian literature, and of her wanderings in the narrow streets behind the Pantheon, where she found her "mysticisme," delighted him, and she had to describe everything at length before he was satisfied. He urged her to read Turgenev, Dowson, and Morris, to ignore Symons (much to her surprise), and to show him all her poems.

In November 1916, six poems by Nancy Cunard, along with poems by seven others, appeared in Edith Sitwell's anthology, *Wheels*. They were her first published poems, and Moore's comment, though flattering, characteristically made demands. "I find that you have written much better poetry than I thought. . . . Nature has given you an exquisite ear for rhythm and I think if things go well with you, you may write some poetry that will do you honour and please your friends." Additional poems appeared in Miss Cunard's first collection, *Outlaws* (1921), which Moore described in the *Observer* as by one possessing "more genius . . . than there is in the great mass of her contemporaries, and much less talent. . . . Genius cannot be acquired; we have it or we have it not; but talent can be." Talent and genius joined two years later in a second collection, *Sublunary* (1923), which displayed a variety of forms and themes and pleased Moore greatly. Yet some dissatisfaction remained, and he wrote: "I am writing to you with delight, for I know that your poems mean a great deal to you, and I don't mean to stint my praise of them; for there is a conviction in my heart of improvement." It was *Parallax*, a free verse poem published in 1925, that rather surprisingly elicited nearly unalloyed admiration from him. Though puzzled at first by the obscurity he finally concluded that "the elusiveness that puzzles today will be tomorrow's delight."

When *Parallax* appeared Nancy Cunard was already a commanding figure in Montparnasse, cosmopolitan, flamboyant, attractive, and talented. Her range of interests had grown enormously since moving to Paris in 1920. Almost at once she had met all the American *émigrés* and formed close friendships with Robert McAlmon, Ezra Pound (whom she was to publish in 1930), and Janet Flanner, and the American artists Man Ray and Eugene MacCown. Curious about whatever was considered avant-garde she was naturally drawn to the work of the dadaists and surrealists, and with several, notably Louis Aragon, René Creval, and Tristan Tzara, her ties became personal as well as intellectual. Of her own countrymen she associated mainly with those who traveled or lived on the Continent, such as Nina Hamnett, the Sitwells, and Norman Douglas. Michael Arlen, portrayed her as the heroine of *The Green Hat,* and Aldous Huxley drew on her for a leading character in *Point Counter Point.* She was painted by Kokoschka, John Banting, Wyndham Lewis; sculptured by Brancusi, and photographed by Man Ray and Cecil Beaton.

References to Nancy Cunard abound in the reminiscences of the twenties and thirties and range from William Carlos Williams's exalted description ("Nancy was to me as constant as the heavens in her complete and passionate inconstancy. Out of passion, to defeat its domination [she] . . . kept herself burned to the bone. What else have the martyrs done?") to Samuel Putnam's more factual appraisal of her as "an honest rebel against her class and what she took to be its narrow outlook . . . who paid the penalty of being some decades ahead of her time." What both authors discerned in her, besides ardor and passion, was action and industry, and the presence of the former always, in her case, produced the latter. Strong objections to the English aristocracy had led to exile and in 1930 prompted a bitter attack (eventually made public) upon her mother and the British upper-class. It estranged her from both. Her horror and disgust upon learning of the suppression of the Negro in the United States led to the making of her *Negro* anthology, and she persuaded her friends Ezra Pound, Theodore Dreiser, Langston Hughes, and Samuel Beckett to contribute selections as part of an effort to focus attention on the Negro dilemma.

Late in 1927 Miss Cunard decided to learn hand-printing. For advice she went to see two old friends, Leonard and Virginia Woolf, who for years had been printing books by hand. They told her her hands would always be covered with ink, which, if intended as an admonition, failed. By the following spring the future home of the Hours Press, a "Cour Normande," at Réanville, Normandy, sixty miles from Paris, had been converted into a printery large enough to house comfortably a bulky, two-hundred-year-old Belgian Mathieu hand-press, which Miss Cunard had bought from Bill Bird, who used it to print his Three Mountains editions of Pound, Hemingway, Williams, and others. The purchase price included a generous amount of Caslon Old Face type, some furnishings, and packages of Vergé de Rives paper; and Bird himself came to Normandy to supervise the installation of the press and even found a French printer skilled in the operation of ancient presses who was willing to teach the novice the secrets of hand-printing.

Miss Cunard learned fast, despite an unexpectedly dull beginning hand-setting what she has since called "that pesky little piece," a *Report on the Pumice-Stone Industry*

of the Lipari Islands for Norman Douglas, who had sent it
to her just as the press opened. When it was finished and in
the mail to Douglas, she turned gratefully to the manuscript that had originally been first on the schedule,
Peronnik the Fool by George Moore. It was G.M., "her
first friend," who, upon learning of her plan to start a
press, had insisted on being the first on the list and sent
her an American edition of *Peronnik*, filled with alterations
and corrections, announcing, "I want to start your press
off with a good bang!"

He succeeded. The two-hundred copies of *Peronnik*
sold out on publication day. The same month, December
1928, Hours printed a Christmas poem for Richard
Aldington, designed he said to get "rid of a lot of rather
tiresome acquaintances," and a month later a four page
poem by the Chilian painter Alvaro Guevara. By the
first of the new year the Hours Press schedule included
The Eaten Heart by Richard Aldington, *One Day* by
Norman Douglas, *XXX Cantos* by Ezra Pound, and
La Chasse au Snark by Louis Aragon. With the addition
of *Mes Souvenirs* by Arthur Symons, and the exception
of Pound's *Cantos*, which was published later, all appeared
before the press moved into Paris in January 1930.

The *anno lucis* of the Hours Press was 1930: a total of ten
volumes was published, including seven collections of
poetry, a selection of essays, a catalogue of paintings, and
a set of six songs with music. Obviously, Miss Cunard was
determined to realize her ambition to publish as much
"contemporary poetry of an experimental kind as
possible." For besides issuing collections by celebrated
poets like Ezra Pound, Roy Campbell, and Robert Graves,
she was publishing work by such "new discoveries" as
Walter Lowenfels, John Rodker, Harold Acton, Brian

Howard, Laura Riding, and, finally, Samuel Beckett. Returning to Paris meant plunging again into the vortex of the art world, which for Miss Cunard remained surrealism. On the walls of the Hours Press printery in Rue Guenégaud, a step from the Galerie Surréalistic, hung paintings by Joan Miró, André Masson, Georges Malkine, and Francis Picabia, and atop the bookcases beneath them stood the strange fetish figures and carvings from Africa and Oceania from which the surrealists had drawn so much inspiration. Among her closest companions at the time were the leaders of *le surréalisme*, André Breton, Louis Aragon, Paul Eluard, and Georges Sadoul, who worked as an assistant at the press for many months. Two surrealists, Man Ray and Yves Tanguy, created covers for Hours Press books; and others were made by the British artist Elliott Seabrooke and the Australian Len Lye.

The end of the Hours came in 1931. Miss Cunard, already for months engaged in collecting material for *Negro,* entrusted the press to a manager until she realized that it could not be operated at a distance. When it became clear that she would have to decide between the press and *Negro*, her choice, no surprise, was *Negro*. By late spring the printery in Rue Guenégaud had closed its doors; the old Mathieu, the type and an assortment of paper and stock were returned to the farmhouse at Réanville, where six years later, at the height of the Spanish Civil War, Miss Cunard dusted them off and printed six *plaquettes* of Spanish war poetry, among which were poems by W. H. Auden, Langston Hughes, Tristan Tzara, and Pablo Neruda.

By a felicitous coincidence the last three books published by the Hours each reflected one of the owner's interests. Bob Brown's *Words* contained verse experiments that, both visually and thematically, challenged the contemporary poetic modes; *The Revaluation of Obscenity* by Havelock Ellis attacked all that Miss Cunard herself opposed: prudery, censorship, hypocrisy; and George Moore's *The Talking Pine*, a dream fragment that the elderly author (he was then nearly eighty) told Miss Cunard on the occasion, so it happened, of their last visit together, excited her love of mystery. The rolling rhythm of the old man's voice that morning in December 1930, sitting in his "breakfast room" in Ebury Street, had never sounded more enchanting, and as he spoke of his dream she visualized it in print. *The Talking Pine* was the final Hours Press publication, and G. M., her "first friend," had become the last of Nancy Cunard's authors.

This record of the Hours Press and of the period in which it existed, unlike the many accounts of the twenties and thirties that concentrate on the lurid and bizarre (Who cares, after all, whether it was Hemingway who knocked Callaghan down, or the other way round?), describes the solid literary achievements of people who for too long have been either dismissed or glorified, depending on the classifier, as a "Lost Generation." What passes as the legend of the Lost Generation, does contain a modicum of fact; but regrettably it is often accepted as the whole truth. Miss Cunard's account may not go far toward changing the story of the Roaring Decade; so durable are legends that have found wide popular appeal. But as the founder and operator of one of the leading expatriate presses she tells another and, to my mind, a vastly more important segment of that story.

It is the story of how books were made, of how ideas

became the words on a printed page, of the creativeness of a small band of book publishers. It is the story of close personal relationships and co-operation between Miss Cunard and the authors she published, which made possible the most fruitful sort of collaboration. Author and publisher conferred during each step of the production of a book, and occasionally even shared the work as well, as when Louis Aragon and Miss Cunard hand-printed the former's translation of Louis Carroll's *The Voyage of the Snark*. It is the story of how books were born, for example, *Henry-Music*. As eager to acknowledge as encourage experimentation, Miss Cunard persuaded her friend Henry Crowder, an American jazz pianist, to collaborate with Samuel Beckett, Richard Aldington, and others in writing music for some of their poems. She oversaw the project herself, and the result, called *Henry-Music*, is perhaps the first occasion when verse has been set to a jazz score. Another time the press sponsored a poetry contest and offered £10 for the best poem on the subject of time. With co-judge Richard Aldington, Miss Cunard read scores of entries, none of them outstanding; then, just as the contest closed, she knew the excitement of making a "literary discovery." The last entry, delivered to the press on the final night of the contest by the author himself, was the winner: it was called *Whoroscope,* and it was signed Samuel Beckett.

These few incidents from the history of the Hours Press reveal that the small private presses could and did cultivate an intimacy between authors and publishers as well as a creative atmosphere that large commercial publishing houses, now as well as then, nearly always lack. Their tradition, however, is kept alive today, but barely, by a few small presses across the country and abroad, but their struggle just to exist is as difficult as that which confronted their predecessors. It is no secret that most expatriate presses had short lives, and the Hours Press was no exception. But what remains impressive is that they accomplished as much as they did, not in numbers, but certainly in quality. Many distinguished names in contemporary literature, names like Hemingway, Pound, Joyce, and Williams, as well as less familiar figures like H. D., Norman Douglas, Bryher, Ford Madox Ford, Mina Loy, and Djuna Barnes owe at least some of their fame as authors to these presses, whose owners were willing to print books by unknown writers which had been, or were certain to be, rejected by established publishers. They encouraged the new and experimental, if not with a promise of publication, then at least with some prospect of it. And that was enough.

Negro, the monumental anthology that forced the closing of the Hours, appeared in 1934. The next several years were undoubtedly Miss Cunard's most productive and, indeed, most exciting, combining as they did a variety of tasks, such as reporting the Abyssinian crisis for the American African Press and the Spanish Civil War for the *Manchester Guardian*; writing poems on Spain and doing literary criticism; and publishing, from Réanville, *Authors Take Sides on the Spanish War* (1937) and the six *plaquettes* of Spanish war poems. In England during the Second World War she alternated between working as a translator for the Free French (she often monitored Ezra Pound's broadcasts from Italy) and writing poetry (*Man-Ship-Tank-Gun-Plane* appeared in 1944 as did her anthology, *Poems for France,* in which she made French translations of poems about France by British poets). She also longed

Foreword

to return to Réanville, and by the time she saw it again in
1945 it had been reduced to a ruin. Gone was most of the
stuff of the Hours: books, letters, manuscripts, art work,
type, and equipment; only the old Mathieu had successfully withstood the foraging of German soldiers and
Norman peasants. Settling again at Réanville seemed impossible; so Miss Cunard went to live in a quiet sector of
southwestern France, near the Dordogne in the region of
Lot, where years before she had traveled with Louis
Aragon.

In 1947 *Poems for France* was reissued in France, and two
years later Miss Cunard brought out *Nous Gens D'Espagne,*
a small collection of poems written after the war. During
the last fifteen years of her life (she died in Paris in March
1965) she turned to biography, writing consecutively
two superb books of remembrances of Norman Douglas
(*Grand Man,* 1954) and George Moore (*G. M., Memories
of George Moore,* 1956); and like them the present volume
combines candid and always lively recollections of her
friends and pieces of a self-portrait, but above all *These
Were the Hours* is the memoir of a press.

Trenton, N.J.   HUGH FORD
July, 1968

xviii

ACKNOWLEDGMENTS

The editor wishes to thank the following for permission to reprint material in this work: Mr. Samuel Beckett for *Whoroscope* and "From an only poet to a shining Whore"; Mr. Robert Graves for "Oak, Poplar, Pine" and "Act V, Scene V."

I should also like to express my thanks for a grant from the American Philosophical Society, which enabled me to travel to France to collaborate with Miss Cunard in the writing of this book.

The following acknowledgment is due to Mr. Gordon Thomson, Deputy Director, National Gallery of Victoria, Melbourne, Australia, for permission to reproduce the portrait of Nancy Cunard by Alvaro Guevara.

CONTENTS

FOREWORD   VII

ACKNOWLEDGMENTS   XIX

ILLUSTRATIONS   XXIII

LA CHAPELLE-RÉANVILLE   3

GEORGE MOORE: *Peronnik the Fool*   17

ALVARO GUEVARA: *St. George at Silene*   31

LOUIS ARAGON: *La Chasse au Snark*   40

RICHARD ALDINGTON: *The Eaten Heart*   51

NORMAN DOUGLAS: *One Day*   59

ARTHUR SYMONS: *Mes Souvenirs*   66

15 RUE GUENÉGAUD, PARIS   74

EUGENE MacCOWN: *Paintings, Drawings*   87
                and Gouaches

WALTER LOWENFELS: *Apollinaire, An Elegy*   92

ROBERT GRAVES: *Ten Poems More*   97
LAURA RIDING: *Twenty Poems Less*

LAURA RIDING: *Four Unposted Letters*   106
              to Catherine

Contents

SAMUEL BECKETT: *Whoroscope*   109

EZRA POUND: *XXX Cantos*   123

ROY CAMPBELL: *Poems*   133

JOHN RODKER: *Collected Poems*   141

HENRY CROWDER: *Henry-Music*   147

RICHARD ALDINGTON: *Last Straws*   156

HAROLD ACTON: *This Chaos*   161

BRIAN HOWARD: *First Poems*   169

BOB BROWN: *Words*   177

HAVELOCK ELLIS: *The Revaluation of Obscenity*   186

GEORGE MOORE: *The Talking Pine*   193

EPILOGUE   195

BIBLIOGRAPHY OF HOURS PRESS PUBLICATIONS   209

INDEX   213

xxii

ILLUSTRATIONS

Peronnik the Fool *title page*   27

Portrait of Nancy Cunard by Alvaro Guevara, 1919   35

The Hours Press list of forthcoming books   55

Exterior of the Hours Press, Paris   77

Eugene MacCown's portrait of Nancy Cunard, 1923   89

Nancy Cunard with her Hours Press books, Spring 1930   101

Nancy Cunard and Henry Crowder in the Hours Press,   113
Paris 1930

Post card announcement of the new address of the   125
Hours Press

The Hours Press list of new works   135

Henry-Music *announcement*   153

Title page from This Chaos *by Harold Acton*   165

THESE WERE
THE HOURS

La Chapelle-Réanville

Late in 1927 I bought a small *Cour Normande,* or farm-house, without land at La Chapelle-Réanville, between Vernon-sur-Seine and Pacy-sur-Eure in Normandy, as remote from Paris as if it were two or three hundred miles away. The "Cour Normande" is generally one long line of house, as was this one, with a barn attached at each end and a mixed lot of lesser buildings facing it around a square or circular space. This charming, rural place belonged to two very old peasants and had cost very little, although the transformation of it was expensive. It seemed to bear no name, but persistent questioning of some of the villagers evoked a vague memory that it had sometimes been known as "Le Puits Carré," or Square Well, and it became that forthwith to me. Sure enough, there was a well, and of such spectacular and difficult depth—30 metres—that an iron ladder had to be affixed within, in view of the constant repairs required by the electric pump at the bottom. How often from the mysterious depth came more trouble than water. The ways of electricity here, a mere sixty miles from Paris, caused many a gnashing-of-teeth interruption to work. Of garden there was scarce anything, nor would there be now that I had decided to learn printing by hand, as done in the old days. Once that began, good-bye to all else, I thought, and afterwards saw I was right.

3

These Were the Hours

Toward the end of spring in 1928, as soon as the house was tolerably finished, I saw that luck had come my way in being able to locate an old hand-press which could be bought on the spot. Of such objects—the more venerable the more difficult to work—there are not ever many on the market. But at that moment William Bird, the well-known newspaperman from the United States, was about to sell his Three Mountains Press, which he had operated at 29 Quai D'Anjou, Ile St. Louis, since 1921. In 1919, Bird and David Lawrence had founded the Consolidated Press Association in the United States and the following year Bird had come to Paris as its general manager. Soon afterward, he realized a long-time ambition: to hand-set and print fine books. In Paris, he met Roger Devigne, who knew well the art of printing by hand, and asked him to teach him the craft. Devigne did and remained to work with Bird at the press. Though Bird financed it himself and regarded the Three Mountains as a hobby, its first six books published in 1923 were indeed artistic achievements. All in the same agreeable tall and narrow format, the six were: *Indiscretions* by Ezra Pound; *Women and Men* by Ford Madox Ford, who incidentally ran his *Transatlantic Review* from an office upstairs at 29 Quai D'Anjou; *Elimus* by B.C. Windeler; *The Great American Novel* by William Carlos Williams; *England* by B.M. Gould Adams; *in our time* by Ernest Hemingway.

A second Hemingway book, *Three Stories and Ten Poems,* actually appeared before the publication of *in our time.* Its publisher was the American writer and poet, Robert McAlmon, who set up his own "publishing house" called Contact Editions at the same address with Bird and began accepting manuscripts. In 1925, Bird

4

himself hand-printed McAlmon's *Distinguished Air*. Ezra Pound, whom I was to publish later, was also closely connected with Bird's operation and became an editor there in 1922. The first printing in book form of any of his cantos (*A Draft of XVI Cantos for the beginning of a Poem of some length*) came out, in 1925, in a sumptuous edition of only ninety copies and was the finest piece of work done at the Three Mountains. But all Bird's volumes had individual character, and if the pressure and inking (always a difficulty with hand-presses) were sometimes irregular, the paper and general taste of the books, embellished with handsome vignettes, were very pleasant indeed.

Thus, what was to become the Hours Press had a distinguished, even an illustrious, lineage and connections. This was an era when private presses flourished, not just in Paris, but at other places on the Continent, in England, and the United States. Ten years before, Leonard and Virginia Woolf had started their Hogarth Press, and from it had come my *Parallax* in 1925; the Beaumont Press came into existence in London in 1917, too, and two years later John Rodker set up the Ovid Press, which began with *Twenty Drawings from the Note-Books of H. Gaudier-Brzeska* (1919), T. S. Eliot's *Ara Vus Prec* (1919), and Ezra Pound's *Hugh Selwyn Mauberly* (1920). Vera and Francis Meynell and David Garnett organized the Nonesuch Press in 1923 and began printing lavish editions of books by classic and modern authors, and in 1926 Jack Lindsay began doing the same at his Fanfrolico Press. About the time I started the Hours, Robert Graves and Laura Riding began their Seizin Press in Hammersmith, from which came the latter's *Love as Love, Death as Death* and Gertrude Stein's *An Acquaintance with*

Description in 1928; their books were nicely designed. Besides being the location of the Bird–McAlmon operation, Paris was the address of Sylvia Beach's Shakespeare and Company, whose huge undertaking it was to bring out *Ulysses*. In 1927, Harry and Caresse Crosby started the Black Sun Press, which was to publish Pound, Crane, Joyce, Kay Boyle, D.H. Lawrence, and Archibald MacLeish. Edward Titus, whose bookshop At the Sign of the Black Manikin was not so well-known as Sylvia Beach's Shakespeare and Company, founded the Black Manikin Press in 1928 and published Mary Butt's *Imaginary Letters* the same year. All of these private presses were, as Janet Flanner has said to me, "proof of the underpinnings of that writing period in Paris, which was only a small part foreign, in quantity, but in influence on the French and indeed everybody in sight, enormous."

How very generous Bill Bird was to me. For £300 not only was it possible to buy the beautiful old Belgian Mathieu press itself, but also a good deal of Caslon Old-Face type, wooden furnishings, and an appreciable amount of paper—a handsome Vergé de Rives. But Bird warned it would be extremely difficult to find mechanics skilled in the task of taking such a press apart and putting it together again, so ancient was the model. So he came to Réanville himself, in April 1928, to supervise the work of re-assemblage. And not only this. The hardest of all was to find a printer who, while proficient as they all had to be with modern presses, still had the complete knowledge of how to manage those of olden times. Bill Bird found such a man, a M. Lévy, who would be my teacher and printer and I was all the more grateful, for it meant that he had agreed to come and work in the country.

The thought of printing had long attracted me, not so

much from the purely aesthetic point of view as from the sense of independent creativeness it might give one. Printing should not, however, be confused with publishing, nor both with distribution. Distribution of one's products is a thing in itself and knowledge of salesmanship is very different from knowledge of type-setting. It is a job apart, although it can be likened to one problem of the writer, or of some writers: that is, more will be written if there be a guarantee that more will be published.

At this first stage, I thought I would like to do mainly contemporary poetry of an experimental kind—always very modern things, short pieces of fine quality that, by their nature, might have difficulty in finding commercial publishers willing to take a chance on them. It was a short-lived idea. Obviously, to restrict oneself to such poetry would be thoroughly uncommercial. At no moment did I envisage my press as a "hobby," any more than it was thought of primarily as a money-making concern. At least, by way of compromise, everything produced should be contemporary. The ideal, as I look back now, would have been for me to print and for someone else to publish, a sympathetic partner who would see eye to eye with me in the choice of works.

But it was as a singlehanded venture that I began Hours in 1928 and ended it in 1931. As for the poetry of an advanced, modern kind which I had thought should be the main characteristic of the Hours, one look at my list of authors, many of them established and already famous, will show how things turned out otherwise. Among the first to be published at Hours were George Moore, Norman Douglas, Arthur Symons, and Richard Aldington; but later came Samuel Beckett, Walter Lowenfels, and Brian Howard. But of this at the beginning, I could have no idea. To be sure, the authors came a little later.

At this time Louis Aragon was much at Réanville and we contemplated learning printing together, or at least type-setting, for neither of us thought of him as becoming something of a printer, which would be the case with me. His writing was too absorbing and important. Founder of surrealism with André Breton, and with him the editor of the intellectual-political review, *La Revolution Surréaliste*, Aragon had little time to spare. There were daily, sometimes twice-daily gatherings in Paris of their group. I have never seen anyone with such concentration as Aragon. He once wrote in front of me a long analytical essay, *Philosophie des Paratonerres*, which he began one evening before dinner and finished some thirty-six hours later, with hardly any time off for sleep or meals. The subject of this 10,000 word criticism was philosophy, stretching from Heraclitus to Spengler, through Marx, Engels, and Dühring. Another example was his *Traité du Style,* a book of medium length, which he planned and wrote to the end in the single month of September, 1927, at Varengeville.

Among friends who knew what I was setting out to do, John Rodker, founder of the Casanova Society, in London, in the 1920's, was encouraging if rather surprised at me. Leonard and Virginia Woolf, whose Hogarth Press had steadily grown in importance, were somewhat otherwise. They too had been hand-setters and worked in the ancient manner. I cannot think they actually wanted to dissuade me, yet I can still hear their cry: "Your hands will always be covered with ink!" This seemed no deterrent. And it was with curiosity I looked at my black and greasy hands after the first go with the inking table. Before me lay my first effort, a short letter to my printer.

La Chapelle-Réanville

Cher Monsieur,
Je crois que c'est bien Samedi prochain que vous devez venir. Comme vous voyez on a commencé à imprimer. Nous avons fait toutes les épreuves du poème, et j'attends un texte. Le matériel va être bientôt expédié.

The smell of printer's ink pleased me greatly, as did the beautiful freshness of the glistening pigment. There is no other black or red like it. After a rinse in petrol and a good scrub with soap and hot water, my fingers again became perfectly presentable; the right thumb, however, began to acquire a slight ingrain of grey, due to the leaden composition. I soon learned that greasy black hands do not matter when one is at the proofing stage, but an immaculate touch is most important in handling the fair sheet when one has reached the pulling stage. This is part of the craft; to achieve impeccably clean things with fingers grease-laden—else there will be a distressing "printer's thumb" in ink on the finished article.

The little "Cour Normande de Puits Carré" possessed a small stable; perhaps it would have been a horse and a cow that were once housed there. This now came in wonderfully well for setting up the press, and a balcony was built inside with shelves for supplies and paper and the drying of the printed sheets. We had good daylight and electric light, and, later, a stove, and it was so near the house, some twenty-five yards away, that I was sometimes tempted, in those early days, to rise from bed and go straight to work. Looking back on the printery I think nothing could have been so well devised for my purpose.

By now the printer, Monsieur Lévy, had arrived and was taking stock rather sourly, I thought, not only of the printery and its contents but of Aragon and myself. He was not an inspiring teacher although a sound one, and doubtless had not yet encountered two such novices as ourselves with our free and easy ways of looking at possibilities, at possibilities, say, of bringing innovations up against some of the consecrated rules of layout, "just for the nice look of the thing."

About this time too came a request from Norman Douglas. "Will you make as faithful a reproduction as you can achieve of my *Report on the Pumice-Stone Industry of the Lipari Islands?*" Douglas had written it originally for the Foreign Office in 1895, and, as he would remark, was "the only meritorious action in my whole life." To undertake the task of writing a report on the pumice-stone industry, a stone, incidentally, used for polishing wood and leather which looks in certain forms like immense, solid rock but is extremely light, Douglas travelled to the Lipari Islands, the principal source of the substance. There he found that the workers, tunnelling frantically like moles inside the mountain till the whole place must have been practically honeycombed with galleries, were fairly well remunerated, but that child labour was fiercely exploited. This was put a stop to entirely, thanks to his *Report*. *Two* lines in this sober official paper on the unhappy use of children as workers was sufficient.

This tightly printed, six-page *Report* was the eye-opener to the mysteries of typesetting and printing and hardly anything could have been more difficult, on account of the various sizes of type and the layout of the cover.

That "pesky little piece," as I frequently called it to myself, had to be set up mostly in 11-point letters, which do not lie easily in the composing stick. Being small, they necessitated much twiddling around by inexperienced fingers, yet I should have to learn to handle them, for next would come George Moore's *Peronnik*, the first book of the Hours, which would be set in the same type. Those who know the difference between 11-point and the very much larger 16-point will appreciate this hard beginning. I do not mean the text. For such is one's absorption—at first especially—that it matters little to the appraising part of one's mind what one is transferring from written or typed pages to what will become the printed page. Sixteen-point, being a much larger letter, is more apt to stay within tactile control at the angle it should than will 11-point. (These were my two main sizes, and proved just right for what was produced.) Such is but one of the beginner's cares. He is soon a little more finger-deft, and gradually very much more so. Meanwhile p's and q's and d's and b's, in all this upside-down-inside-out world of printing, begin to acquire or resume their proper individuality, and of course "minding one's p's and q's" comes from printing terminology. In all, I thought, hand-setting was like sewing, one stitch at a time; one must *like* doing either to attain proficiency.

A little grim, all the same, was *Pumice*, by reason of its dry, conventional style and content. It seemed at first as if it were going to be hard to make "as exact a copy as possible," so temperamental did the old hand-press prove to be at times. The niceties of the complicated cover were left to Monsieur Lévy, who acquitted himself admirably, to the delight of Douglas on receiving the replica.

About half of *Pumice* is my composition and it was turned out at the end of fifteen days or so. At the same time things were being put in order in the printery and Aragon and I were also trying our hands a little at setting up a few lines of *Peronnik*. The original of the *Report* had to go back to Douglas, it being the only copy he possessed.

Our edition, a small present to him, although he offered to pay me, was a mere eighty copies, enough for him to distribute to friends and collectors of his complete works. In view of the benefits derived later from his *One Day* it was a fit little present. I remember a letter full of astonishment from Douglas at its having been possible to make such a good replica, along with a suggestion that I visit him in Italy when there later in the summer.

It became clear little by little that Monsieur Lévy was a *pince-sans-rire*, who thought of himself as a dry wit. Wry, all wry did he seem to us in his views on life. An ex-anarchist, he told me he was, an *ex*, and this somehow meant that he was disgruntled at much.

His surprise was great at our learning to handle type so fast. Yet it seemed to me that anyone who likes doing this at all must acquire the feel of it the first or certainly the second time he brings the *composteur* or printing-stick together with the letters; a few hours are sufficient to get the feel of it all. Aragon and I were both fairly quick at composition from the start. Learning the correct sequence, or rather non-sequence, alphabetically, of the compartments where each letter is kept in its scores and hundreds, is another matter and takes somewhat longer. We were soon decent apprentices. With neither occurred any catastrophic collapses of lines or paragraphs when tipping out the *composteur*; our pages could be tied up almost as well as if set by a professional. Distributing the type after printing four pages or so was pleasant and not the bore it is considered to be by printers, and everything about the craft seemed to me most interesting.

Our enthusiasm caused Monsieur Lévy to become disgruntled. Another printer might have rejoiced, but not he. Novices should not be thus, it was all wrong. Usually there are cascades of type and cries of wrath at having to clear up and start all over again, with loss of time and a sense of ashamedness.

"In France," said he, "one can't be a printer, you know, unless one has worked a long time."

"How long?"

"Seven years."

"Oh! And what is all that stretch filled with?"

"Well, first of all you are made to sweep the floor and pick up fallen type and pieces. You're only a lad, they shouldn't let you get your hands on composing. You keep the place tidy, run errands and so on. Then, little by little, you're permitted to learn to set type, and all the rest comes later. It depends on your intelligence, it's a lengthy job."

"Thank goodness there's none of that here, Monsieur Lévy! We are going to forge ahead. My intention is to learn from you everything I possibly can as quickly as may be, so as to be able to work without you as well as with you, do you see? I like this beginning very much."

"And then," said he, "you and Monsieur Aragon are about to fly in the face of accepted conventions and long-established rules, all of them! This projected layout of yours is not at all in conformity with . . ."

"Monsieur Lévy, consider this an experimental place whenever you are going to think of conventional rules. See what difficulty we are having with my first circular, on account of the many different sizes of letters. So much has *got* to go on the first page, and such and such must stand out in order of importance. This is the problem: how to fit things in together, so many of them, and yet make a nice looking, not overfull page. How can old rules not come into conflict with such things at times? Taste, Monsieur Lévy, taste! Not so often does one find it in purely commercial printing. I want, also, innovations, though I am not out for them with this circular, it is much too difficult as it is. But things must *look* nice. Innovations, by all means, in our books. They make for the individuality of any press that is not commercial. A new vision, no matter how nonconformist, will also suit the character of some of the things that are going to be produced here."

Now and again Aragon's dark eyes would flash or laugh at me behind Monsieur Lévy's hefty shoulder. Why waste talk on the man who would never understand or agree? he seemed to be saying.

Two important matters had to be settled early. One was the amount of royalties to be offered each author; the other was the publicity for Hours. I decided that my terms to authors would be one-third of the proceeds of sales, after deducting costs of production, or 33 per cent, which I thought a good deal more than the average 10 or 15 per cent in general use. In the case of George Moore and Norman Douglas, authors so famous they could expect higher royalties, it was 50 per cent after cost deduction, or half the gain. My general production expenses were at this time very low, no rent being paid of course for the printery, as it belonged to me. In a large, black ledger, I noted on one page the cost of every successive book, such as printer's time, light, heat, paper, binding, postage, and a small percentage of the expenses of circulars and their postage—and that was all. On the opposite page were entered orders, addresses, and payments. There is a great deal to be said for doing things oneself, by one's own system.

Not one arrangement had been made at the start for the distribution of the books when issued, save a fair-sized list of possible individual buyers and patrons. The first circular, however, demanded that those who received them should be able to know where to procure my volumes in London, New York, Paris, and Florence, or otherwise than by writing to me directly. Thus I listed the Warren Gallery, in London, owned and run by Dorothy Warren, the Holliday Bookshop in New York, Edward Titus, 4 Rue Delambre, Montparnasse, Paris, and Pino Orioli, 6 Lungarno Carsini, Florence. It had been Norman Douglas's advice that not more than ten per cent discount be given booksellers, and he pointed out that, in view of the small number of each edition, this was perfectly fair. Despite a little demur at this on the part of some of the trade, I will say the booksellers, particularly those in London, were gratifyingly prompt in their response to my circulars, as were later some of those in provincial English towns. Advance orders worked well, especially for the Norman Douglas and George Moore volumes. And prompt payment is also to the credit of the booksellers and most of my clients. At this early time I had no book-traveller and was unable to tell how to make the best use of publicity, as advertising in reviews seemed to be somewhat disproportionate in cost, although on some occasions I did advertise some of the books. This first circular listed the following books, all of which I planned to turn out in about eight months: *Peronnik the Fool* by George Moore, *St. George at Silene* by Alvaro Guevara, *The Hunting of the Snark* by Lewis Carroll and translated into French by Louis Aragon, *The Eaten Heart* by Richard Aldington, *The Probable Music of Beowulf* by Ezra Pound, *One Day* by Norman Douglas, *A Canto* by Ezra Pound, and *A Plaquette of Poems* by Iris Tree.

Contrasting with the great pleasure I found in setting type and, tempered with criticism, in holding the first bound volume of each book in my hands as it came from the binders, is the memory of being introduced to "permanent fatigue." Back-breaking as well as wrist-breaking is typesetting, but I soon found a palliative in doing my composing seated on a high bar-stool. My printer scoffed at such refinement. Typesetters are ever up and about a printery looking for various letters, it was explained; custom orders them to stand up to their eight-hour day— at least in France. I had never done regular working-hours before save as a child at day-classes, and the self-discipline of work was something to be learned. Although I was my own master, it was obvious that regularity must be established and maintained, else how would anything get done on time? "It's always twice as long as you think" is an echo I would like to pass on. But approximately well done to time was the work. One must like what one is doing to be able to give that extra effort which gets swallowed up in the final result. Gradually, however, the work became engrossing and, quite soon, it turned into a fourteen or fifteen hour day.

Before long two things began to take away time from the printery: the large amount of correspondence that developed, and the keeping of accounts. In my surge towards composing I had not thought of either, and each greatly added to the work of the "firm," which of course consisted but of the printer and myself. Had I taken counsel from some already established private press, I believe the conventional way of doing things, which would probably have been part of their advice, would have put me off. Good authors (in several cases very famous ones), hard work, luck, and ignorance of the usual complexities in publishing were certainly the three pillars of the Hours during its first year.

George Moore

Peronnik the Fool

The real beginning of work by the Hours Press, that is to say its first book, was George Moore's *Peronnik the Fool*, a long short story. First written for his lengthy and beautiful novel, *Héloïse and Abelard*, as the tale told by Héloïse to her small son Astrolabe, thinking it would help him regain the French he had lost during his years in Brittany, it seemed later to Moore to be too long a digression. Self-critical and ever revising and rewriting as he was, he decided it would interrupt the flow of the narrative in the book, and such was the reason for its appearing on its own, a legend told to a boy.

It had been published in New York the year before, in a private edition of 785 copies, designed by Bruce Rogers and printed at the press of William Edwin Rudge, Mount Vernon, with a somewhat medieval look to it, a pleasant little volume. And now George Moore (or "G. M." as he was always known) wanted me to do it. The American edition he sent me contained a good number of alterations and corrections which, said he, were of enough consequence to amount to something for collectors of his works. I recall G. M.'s beaming smile and his encouraging words: "I want to start your press off with a good *bang!*" How unlike Moore's generally impeccable diction was that very peculiar word "bang."

How kindly, and also how trusting it was to give this work to a novice who had as yet done nothing to show how she might develop as a printer. Obviously *Peronnik* would have to be carefully produced, not only from my own point of view, but from his, and would we agree? G. M. was most particular about the *taste* which went into these small, signed, limited editions of his works, and I wonder if he was not the first, or among the first, to publish in such costly fashion.

Pumice finished and sent off, M. Lévy and I (for Aragon had gone to Paris) now set to with *Peronnik*. Sufficient paper was at hand for the work, that pleasing Rives which the generous Bird had thrown in with the press and equipment. After some quick calculation the printer estimated that the book would probably come to between sixty and seventy pages. It seems this was one of those occasions when the French, who so often are astonishingly vague about matters which should be exact, suddenly became very precise. I do believe M. Lévy actually wanted me to count the words in the story one by one, instead of in the English way, by figuring the average words to a line on the page.

G. M. had written to me in September to suggest that *Peronnick* would sell quickly if I wrote a preface recounting my youthful memories of him when he was much at Nevill Holt, the country home where I was born and lived as a child.

If you wish to make certain of selling the whole edition quickly (he wrote) you have only to write a preface, and the subject of that preface should be Holt. I wish you would turn those past times over in your mind; spend an evening or two with the subject, and perchance it may flash into your mind in literary form. The story is a very living one and will delight everybody as much as it delights you when I remind you of ... I stop without having said all, leaving the selection of the subject-matter to you.

Of course, a preface of the kind I suggest would cause that cheerless soul, T.S. Eliot, to frown, but personal literature, as I have often impressed upon you, is the only literature for the age it is written and for the age that follows. It isn't easy, however, and it has to be cultivated.

The idea made me quail. I could not have written anything then to accompany his measured prose, and, besides, I had decided that I must devote my energy entirely to printing. I wrote to G.M. "the learning of printing has engulfed me entirely; you cannot imagine how every hour of the day goes into it, but such *is* the case, dearest G.M." The subject lay tactfully unmentioned in the letters we then enchanged, and I felt certain his book would go forth better unprefaced. Many years later, however, his wish returned to me, and I wrote about his many visits to Holt in my book *G.M., Memories of George Moore*.

By now I had mastered typesetting sufficiently to do it unaided, and could even disregard—being accustomed to it—the feeling that one's wrist was breaking from the weight of the five leaden lines in the *composteur*. Moreover, I could be certain there would be no mishaps in the handling of type, which often comes from inexact setting, and that my lines would not be loose. When loose, the letters tend to slope in the printing-stick or on the tray. The first time this happened M. Lévy shot off one of his quips (it must be a classic to printers in France) when I pointed out that my line must be wrong somewhere. But how?

"Of course. Your letters are going to lie down."

"But why?"

"Must be tired, I expect!"

I began to learn that letters are one thing, and a mass of type something else to be thought over in relation to the space to be printed *and* the unprinted space surrounding it. It seemed to me, however, that the chances of printing a fair page were good if you had thought about these matters rightly. Every bit as important in the total aspect is the non printed as well as the printed surface; it was their relation to each other that I found difficult to attain at first and indeed for some time. Vital, too, I discovered, are the vertical spaces between words: the easy 6-point, 4-point, and 3-point, the more slender 2-point and the tenuous 1-point—even the tiny, copper hair-point space can all make a difference. Perfect precision of fit must invest hand-setting, and it takes some learning. As for the other spaces, the leaden and wooden ones that go horizontally, the wooden "furniture," the choice of them must also be tasteful. Any misjudgment of these materials can make the difference between what one might call a good, or even a "noble" page, and one that looks ordinary or even mingy. Everyone knows that a title-page, full of letters and spaces of different sizes, is a hard thing to design. And in this regard my thoughts were often with G. M., for his insistence on beautiful title-pages was well known, his taste always excellent—simple and distinguished at the same time.

We had not so very much type and after we had printed four pages we had to stop and distribute it at once so that we had enough for the next fold. *Peronnik* was done in pulls of four pages at a time, with the other four on the reverse of the same sheet. Here M. Lévy got back at me for my quickness at typesetting. The ways of pagination entirely baffled me; I could not manage the calculation of this head-to-headness and back-to-backness within the compass of a mere eight pages. This need not have troubled me, for one had merely to copy the sequence of the first lot printed: pp. 8-1-5-4—2-7-3-6, and *in quarto*. But he enjoyed his moment of triumph and explained this seemingly complicated procedure with a patronizing hauteur.

But it was during a five-day solitude while M. Lévy was away that I convinced myself I could become a printer. Working alone in a heat-wave which made more tricky yet the right consistency of the paper that had to be dampened and the preparation of the inking, I set and printed the second lot of four pages. I remember feeling glad that G. M. was not there to watch me, because I wanted him to know only the finished product, and yet it would have amused and interested him to see the making of a book, by a novice, on an ancient hand press. He might also have been alarmed about the final result. No, it was best to be alone at this while the printer was away. Counting the two hundred odd sheets, all printed at the end of the day, was gratifying. Single-handed I was doing the work of two, even of three, for the perfect rhythm should go thus: one for the inking table and inking of the composition, another for doing the margining—that is, setting the paper just right above the type and a third for the actual printing, applying the pressure by means of the long lever. To do all this alone was extremely slow. There were some extra sheets, too, that should go to G. M as proofs; they would show him the paper of the edition and also the format; they would be like a slice of the book itself.

Great heat will do odd things to ink and paper and the

Vergé de Rives had to be well dampened before printing; I feared it would dry before I could deal with all the sheets. And that rich, black pigment in its tube, spread it on as one did in daily fashion, the heat might evaporate the added drops of petrol all too fast. Being alone in that temperature of 95 degrees F. or so, I was working in my shift, and thus moved about more easily. I worried about the uneven pressure of the old Mathieu. It is one of those things that are forever being tinkered with, and, in despair at a few of the sheets heavily indented with pressure at top or bottom, I seemed to hear G. M.'s voice floating over the Channel to me: "Come now! This is not printing, this is Braille!"

For all that, "Braille" would have been an exaggeration. And when he wrote me about those pages it was nothing of the kind, but to praise them. However, the "gutter" displeased him.

I hope you understand that I do not consider this imposition the only imposition, but it is the basis from which most impositions spring, and when I saw so much gutter in the first specimen that you sent me I felt it to be my duty to beg of you to take note that in all the 17th and 18th century books a beautiful spacing was always the printer's first consideration.

Nor had a try or two at the title-page pleased him. These objections I dealt with as best I could. The gutter had to remain but ended by not disturbing him, and three or four new attempts at the title-page won his approbation, so that one of them was quickly chosen.

About a month's work was put in on *Peronnik* before the printer went away for the long summer holidays. It was agreed that he should return in the autumn with a contract for several months, as long as it would take to produce all the books I had listed in my catalogue. It now seemed very clear that hand-setting and hand-printing were extremely lengthy matters, a thing one had always heard said. Experience of this, however, is necessary, to show just how lengthy.

By the time I returned from Italy, where I had stayed a few days with Norman Douglas in his delicious apartment on the Lungarno, in Florence, it was November. At this time Douglas was producing, with Pino Orioli at his Lungarno editions, a good number of his own books. In 1928, it was his marvelously funny, scatological *Some Limericks*. Time and again he demonstrated, with figures to back him up, how printing private editions was the way to make money, at least the only way in which he could. He worked very hard. Selling was ensured by an enormous list of private subscribers. His day was hardly long enough for the endless correspondence, the packing and registering of the books, all of which he did himself. He also supervised the printing, and it was surprising that Italian typesetters, without any knowledge of English, should have been able to turn out books so free of errors. However, into one of those he gave me, he had written: "57 typographical errors *here*," and it was then he handed me the typescript of *One Day* to publish.

Return to Réanville was dire. Winter had come with gaunt strides and most of the house was freezing. But the printery was warm, which was slightly troublesome, for the fumes of the stove would now and again make M. Lévy and me droop over our work. Daylight was short; the dreadful interruptions in the electric current now began; and I was sometimes despondent, alone now in the house (for the printer lodged in the village), with a couple of gawky French servants.

Gales of wind and horrible cold accompanied the resumed work on *Peronnik*, but there would be a good moment in the morning when the post arrived, bringing more orders and even a cheque or two in advance. Worst at this time were the *pannes d'électricité*, leaving us literally poised in the dark, all in one moment, as like as not pulling a four-page sheet. To do such precise work by anything but electricity seemed out of the question, although, to be sure, it was done thus in the past. And one always kept on hoping those branches which had come down on the line somewhere, interrupting the current, might be lopped off once and for all.

A letter arrived from G. M. lamenting that he could not come and visit me, see the press, "and walk round your little domain with you." At the age of seventy-seven or so then, he was ill enough at that moment to be tied to Ebury Street. The thought of G. M. at Réanville, in such temperatures and conditions, made me almost shudder. What would he have found? Icy draughts in the nice but uncomfortable house. No steaming cups of tea in a warm room over literary conversation at the regular hour, for work in the printery would see to that. No leisurely walks through wooded glades such as we had known in past summers. No smiles of attainment in me, more likely a worried frown.

He would have liked the dark green painted press in the small outhouse, for the Mathieu was nearly two hundred years old, and he would have admired the great counterweight to the lever in the shape of a classical Empire lamp set atop. The matter of getting exactly the right amount of pressure on the page would have interested him, as would the precision there has to be in *la marge*— the margining—and the setting of the sheet just right to *le blanchet,* to avoid the presence of that extraordinary little phenomenon known as *le frisage. Le frisage* would have appealed much to his love of detail and craftsmanship and would have absorbed him passingly. It is a series of small curlicues of ink that a puff of air, at the moment pressure is applied, creates around part of the type on a page. He would have wanted to know the name of everything in English as well, and I could not have told him. And why a *cicero*? A narrow strip of wood is called a *cicero.* And then, possibly, the light would have gone off, the current having been cut maybe for three hours or even for three days, not only in the printery but in the house and hamlet as well.

No, I doubt that any enthusiasm he might have felt would not have failed him, as it sometimes did me. All might have ended with a testy exclamation: "Why *do* you try to work in such circumstances, my dear Nancy? It cannot be done!"

The speed we kept up at *Peronnik* was good and regular. I wanted the book to come out just before Christmas, and this we achieved to time. The binding was done in Paris, and although I explained very carefully what was desired, the binders turned out a slightly unconvincing volume. Now why is this? It is due, mainly, to the type of letters used for the title, stamped in gold on the cloth covers. The book was bound in pale blue cloth of the same shade as that of the privately printed editions of George Moore in blue with vellum–like spines, and this was satisfactory. *Peronnik* pleased G. M. He had been a model of speed in returning me the pages with his signature, and wrote me his appreciation of the work, and to my mother he said, "The edition is printed on beautiful rag paper, the finest I have ever seen."

These Were the Hours

A little before Christmas, 1928, when *Peronnik* was almost finished, a welcome addition came to the Hours in the person of an enchanting aide and companion, an Afro-American musician, Henry Crowder, whom my cousins, Edward and Victor Cunard, and I had met in Venice the previous summer. The three of us had gone to the Hotel Luna for supper and dancing and had had the unexpected pleasure of hearing the thrilling music of "Eddie South's Alabamians" and then meeting Eddie, "the dark angel of the violin," Mike, the huge black guitarist, Romie, the drummer, and Henry. We saw much of these charming, elegant American musicians, and after they had moved on to Paris for more cabaret work and Henry had grown tired of the exhausting schedule, I urged him to come and work at the Hours, in a general way. He accepted. By now the amount of clerking, as we called the billing and circularising, account-keeping and correspondence, was taking away much of my time from the printery. Henry, I thought, could assist me with this work, as well as in the printery. My hopes were soon realised, for Henry quickly learned to manipulate the press lever, and it was three of us who finished the last pages of *Peronnik* at an accelerated rhythm.

Henry, an excellent pianist, was a great deal more than a jazz musician; he was a born‹teacher, I should say, or at least he became that now as he introduced me to the astonishing complexities and agonies of the Negroes in the United States. He became my teacher in all the many questions of color that exist in America and was the primary cause of the compilation, later, of my large *Negro Anthology*. But at this time I merely listened with growing indignation to what he had to tell: of the race riots and lynchings, the segregation in colleges and public

PERONNIK
THE FOOL

BY

GEORGE MOORE

(Revised Edition)

The Hours Press
Chapelle-Réanville, Eure, France
1928

Peronnik the Fool title page

places, the discrimination that was customary in all aspects of life. It was to this I would return after long afternoons in the printery working with M. Lévy. Henry would have been practising the piano and playing for hours, and it was to the strains, now thundering and dramatic, now romantic and plangent, of Gershwin's *Rhapsody in Blue*, floating out on the wind, that the first book of the Hours was finished.

Henry also drove the car on our numerous posting expeditions to Vernon and Paris. Of all things, he had started his youth in the U.S. postal service, and this somehow meant that he was an expert packer. It was he who taught me the right length of string to compute per package and the size of wrapping paper to prepare for one or more books. He was invaluable to the Hours in a dozen ways, and there was much laughter between us on account of his sometimes shrewd, sometimes naïve observations "on all the men and matters concerned." Addressing envelopes was also part of his work and I remember the start with which I first saw words like these: Sir Ralph Faggotson Esq.

It would have taken too long to explain the *why* of the correct way of addressing the aristocracy. All that was necessary was to make certain that no *Esq.* should henceforward follow a *Sir*, and in this Henry immediately concurred, saying it meant not the slightest difference to him; all that he wanted was to be sure of giving "good service." The string and paper flew through his expert hands, and thereby was removed an earlier apprehension of mine: how to pack in two days, in three at most, some two hundred or more books, all of which would have to be registered, which in France is never the easy thing it is in England.

By publication day *Peronnik* had sold all its two hundred copies, an extra twenty-five being those for the author and for review. I remember praise in the reviews, but only the comments made in the *Times* remain at hand. There the reviewer complimented Moore's "concrete details," saying they gave the "myth a genuine and unsophisticated quality," and his style which in his words assimilated the "fantastic details of a medieval romance."

Alvaro Guevara

St. George at Silene

The second production of the Hours was very agreeable to do, very agreeable indeed. It was a poem by a young, already well-known Chilean painter, Alvaro Guevara, on the legend of St. George and the Dragon.

Guevara lived much in England and was for years at the well-known art school, the Slade. Like his famous South American compatriot, le Comte de Lautréamont, he had a mythology or symbology of his own. In other, later writings he might be called a surrealist, although this was not at all the case in his painting. I do not think Guevara was a tragic figure as was certainly the author of *Les Chants de Maldoror,* Lautréamont. A sarcastic one, rather. His irony was interspersed with pleasant pieces of naïveté, which may have come from the fact that very Spanish, or rather Chilean, did he remain. Now simple, now complex, now direct, now devious, those astonishing verbal images of his would often come out on the wings of mumbled fantasy. And his imagination. Who could properly follow whither it seemed to lead? Well as I knew him, he startled even me once, and how much more so Michael Arlen, during a long monologue, by asking us if Dostoevsky did not appear somewhat in the light of "a carthorse in a bowler hat." Saying this he may have had one book of Dostoevsky's in mind, and one alone. Arlen's scandalized expression was enough for the conversation to turn towards less rarified remarks, around the *vin rouge ordinaire* we were drinking that night in such full measure. I feel the analogy might have led somewhere if properly, that is, lengthily, pursued.

The English of Guevara, or "Chile" as he was ever known to us, was excellent, but it had a sort of "plus" quality about it that was remarkable to hear on many an occasion, and if his thoughts flew at times in dizzy gyration they were also often soberly subtle. I can remember no giddy soarings when it came to discussions of painting. On those occasions he was the serious artist and was much esteemed as such, and as a friend, by Augustus John and Wyndham Lewis, to name but two.

In 1914, with my friend, Iris Tree, then also a student at the Slade School, I met Chile for the first time. It was in the Eiffel Tower restaurant in London, just off Tottenham Court Road, which owed its fame to Augustus John who, twenty years before, had discovered the place and turned it into an artist's rendezvous. The menu, printed in French, sported a cover by Wyndham Lewis, and at the bottom appeared a note describing the Eiffel Tower's very special dining rooms: the Vorticist Room, a special private room with paintings and ornamentations by Mr. Wyndham Lewis, and the Vorticist Anti-Room, with paintings and ornamentations by Mr. William Roberts. Seeing Chile there for the first time, I was nonplussed by the tall, rather slouchy South American dressed in a black suit somewhat short in the arm. But I was struck by his fine, sensitive hands which he always kept thrust deep into his pockets as he shambled down streets, with, of all things, a bowler hat on his fine, massive head. It was not long before I realised that my first impression had been wrong. I saw revealed in his pale face an artist suggestive of fine quality, and how thoughtful a one as well. I admired his tenacity, his often madly argumentative nature, and the resoluteness with which he went about his work. In 1919, Chile's sincerity became all the more evident during some long winter weeks while he was painting the full-length portrait of me, now in the National Gallery of Victoria, in Melbourne, Australia. Hours of silence would slip away as the day drooped into December murk. Then, stopping, he would read me as like as not a poem he had just written, and I would think how much of a painter's poem it was— each thing in its place, full of color, as if seen and created there. Now and again appeared an obscurity, yes; but never one due to loose thinking, rather to some personal twist of words. The perspective, too, was very individual, and that word recalls how upset was many a critic by the perspective in his splendid portrait of Edith Sitwell, since a good number of years in the Tate Gallery. It seems to me it was already there in 1919, but if it reached the Tate only a few years later, this in itself was a high honor for a painter still in his early twenties, in those days particularly. How well this portrait of Edith has aged in forty years. How striking it is in tone now, possessing the same pristine vitality, and already bearing the stamp of permanence.

Fascinated by music halls, boxing rings, swimming pools, and circuses, Guevara did many paintings and drawings of them while in England, besides a number of portraits, including rather well known ones of Ronald Firbank and the Viscountess Curzon. And then he vanished to Chile for a long time. We met again on his return and, knowing by then that I was interested in ethnography, he gave me a very fine present: no less than two of the over-life-size stone heads that are found on Easter Island, which he had picked up for nothing in Valparaiso. Later, married to the beautiful Meraud Guinness, herself a fine painter, he lived much in Paris and Provence. His last exhibition in England, in November 1952, at the Mayor Gallery in London, was, alas, posthumous. Partly retrospective, it contained paintings of different periods; the more recent work in black and white made one appreciate how his style had changed and had developed in a new direction.

Chile had given me *St. George at Silene* during the 1914–18 war. It is a poem-fresco, a rambling fresco. If this seems a contradiction in terms, because it can be argued that things in a painting may be seen at once, being all there confronting the eye, it can be maintained that many a painting will not develop within one's sense otherwise than gradually. Many unfold their subject little by little; for instance, Orcagna's *Triumph of Death*, before its destruction by war in the Campo Santo of Pisa, could certainly not be taken in all at once.

From the first reading of it until today, *St. George* has seemed to me contemporary in feeling with Benozzo Gozzoli, as authentic as some fifteenth-century Italian mural. Even unknowingly, Guevara might have put some pre-Raphael feeling for color and detail into it, but there is not a trace of such in the spare and sometimes (but not displeasingly) naïve lines. Tuscany in flower under spring skies arises around the tender and violent narrative in verse. To Ezra Pound, too, writing of *St. George* in *The Dial*, came the feeling of Italy before the Renaissance. "Senor Guevara has dug up the secret of the pre-Renaissance; he has heard of St. George as Carpaccio presumably heard of him. By simple ignorance of all criteria of English

Portrait of Nancy Cunard by Alvaro Guevara, 1919

verse he writes with real naïveté at a time when the grovel-
ling English are breaking their backs to attain the false.
The secret of the pre-Renaissance, of Simone Martini, for
example, is interest in the main subject of a composition,
the decadence, culminating in Gongorism, is perfection
of detail, or attention to detail and oblivion of the first aim.
I doubt if any skilled poet could deal with a saint's legend
without boring the reader intolerably; Senor Guevara
will merely infuriate the clever. . . . Were I called upon
to explain why this poem is readable I should ascribe it to
the fact that the author is a well-known painter and that
the habit of discipline in his own art has given him the
fundamentals of aesthetic in another, so that his clichés and
inversions do not almightily matter; if he had faked he
would have ruined the whole thing, but there is no touch
of pretentiousness or precosity; his artifice is rhyme,
always very simple, and utterly without inhibition."

Ezra's praise delighted me, for I too felt that the strength
of *St. George*, its admixture of the fierce and tender, came
from his curious mind, the way he fixed his vision, as well
as his remoteness from contemporary poetic trends.
Although *Peronnik* had yet to be finished, I also wanted
St. George to be ready for Christmas, and therefore I took
on the job of setting the four large pages of the "plaquette"
myself. At times temperamental with *Peronnik*, the
Mathieu behaved admirably with this poem, no doubt
because its generous format suited the press so well. The
16-point Caslon stood out boldly on the handsome Velin
de Rives paper. To my mind, poetry should be printed in
large, well-spaced type, this being the one that dresses and
best does it justice. Printing covers and end papers tripled
the labor, and lengthened what I thought would be a quick
job. Chile's cover designs on strong grey paper form

37

rows of small red leaves, between which appear the title and the author's name. Inside, the end paper opposite the title of the poem repeats the leaf motif; however the leaves spread across the final end paper are weeping copious tears. How completely Chile tried to visualize his theme.

A distinguished guest now appeared from Paris on some business for Norman Douglas. He was John Mavrogordato. Few were the visitors during those printing days, but I was enchanted to see this one. I cannot imagine it was the first time he had seen a hand press at work, yet John's interest was genuine and spontaneous. So this was pulling-day . . . and that meant that nothing could stop for longer than lunch, while inking and printing were going on? Exactly. The rhythm should not be broken and it would be absurd to start on something so long and consecutive for a mere hour or two; besides, the inking, which must always be as meticulous as possible, dries overnight. Swathed in a rug in the draughty little place—he had missed his train back to Paris—the courteous man sat a long time as M. Lévy and I bent over our work, now and then handing him a fresh sheet for inspection. Can anyone have ever read a mere title so often? That day we were printing *St. George at Silene* and nothing else.

"Stitching and stabbing" are binders' terms and it was interesting later on to see the deft way the *brocheuses*, or stitchers, were assembling and dealing with one of my books preparatory to the covers being put on. Before machinery for this existed, it must have been an unending job done by hand. The simple sewing of the pages of *St. George* into their covers was a pleasure to me, and an advantage as well, for it took relatively little time and was begun and finished without any of the delays one had to get accustomed to at the binders.

38

Alvaro Guevara

As my Christmas deadline for *Peronnik* and *St. George*
approached, with Henry, M. Lévy, and me performing
multiple tasks so as to finish on schedule, an urgent request
came from Richard Aldington, whom I had met in Rome
for the first time the previous October, for 150 copies of a
special Christmas message he wished to send to his friends.
Somehow I managed to set the type for *Hark the Herald*,
which was Aldington's title, print the 150 copies, and
return them to him in time for Christmas mailings.
Though no doubt capable of offending many, the little
"satire on Christmas greetings," which Aldington has
called it, was amusing and succeeded, in his words, in
"getting rid of a lot of rather tiresome acquaintances."

Louis Aragon

La Chasse au Snark

The elements that attracted the first surrealists (that is, the real ones, those of France) and were incorporated into their domain were remarkably disparate. This group of thirty or so young men, several of whom were painters and the rest writers and poets, was a granite core in the circle of sympathizers and those actively influenced by them, which could sometimes, and sometimes not, be called "the outer circle." The core—and how creative it was—wrote, painted, and signed collective manifestoes, and met for discussion in the same Paris café at least daily and often twice a day. One of their year-long centers was the Café Cyrano, Place Blanche, in Montmartre.

Highly and lavishly productive was *le Surréalisme*; its main leaders were the writers André Breton, Louis Aragon, Paul Eluard, René Crevel, Philippe Soupault, Robert Desnos, Benjamin Péret, and the painters Yves Tanguy, André Masson, Georges Malkine, but there were also many others who signed the leaflets and appeals, including Salvador Dali at times, Joan Miró, and the American painter and photographer Man Ray. *Le Surréalisme* would be easier to define if so many things, principally writings, had not come into it. Personally, I think it is quite impossible to "explain," though someone may be able, years hence, to write concise articles on it for some as yet non-existent encyclopaedia of the many movements in arts and letters. However *avant-garde* should be a first word in any definition. But what words should follow, to give the right idea of the aims and developments of this far-more-than-a-movement revolution? An intellectual revolution it certainly was, which, as such, began in 1924–25.

There was *le côté noir* to it (Edgar Allan Poe was one of the authors held in great esteem); a blend of mystery, imagination, and the miraculous. The suicide of young men, either from postwar despair, the despair of an artist or of a man who could not bear his inability to express himself fully, was in a sense honored, as were love and emotion, and inventiveness and fantasy. The most admired writings were revolutionary, not only in a social-political sense, but in the aesthetic-iconoclastic one too. Writings on psychoanalysis and studies of the subconscious inspired as much as Bosch, Breughel, Archimboldo, Rimbaud, Apollinaire, and de Lautréamont. As creative and experimental as either Picasso and Picabia, with whom they had so many links, the surrealists at the same time railed against many of the consecrated values, though by no means all, for what about Zola, who was another admiration of theirs? Anatole France's death and public funeral provoked a denunciatory sheet called *Avez-vous jamais giflé un cadavre?* And true it was that on and off came waves of *le scandale pour le scandale.* And some artists of whom it was felt that they had betrayed their aesthetic integrity to box-office commercialism were castigated.

All the jingo values of *La Patrie* and *La Gloire*, the militarism so real to official France, were anathematised, and colonialism was consistently denounced. At one time all the group signed a protest against the continuation of the war against Abd-el Krim in the Spanish Moroccan Riff. Ethnography, the study of sculpture, carving, and other handmade objects once thought of as the work of mere "savages" from ancient Africa, Oceania, and of the Indians of both the Americas, were greatly admired and prized, and several of the surrealists eventually became expert ethnographers from their sheer love of such things. Among these were especially Aragon, Breton, Eluard, and Sadoul, while Michel Leiris, at the time one of the most fiery of the writers, has been (since many years now) the Director of Black Africa at Le Musée de l'Homme in Paris.

There was *la période des sommeils*, during which several of the surrealists (René Crevel was one of the best at this) went into a sort of trance and spoke aloud the thoughts or images that came through their subconsciousness, which were taken down, and occasionally published. One may imagine how much of a *non sequitur* such writing represented to part of the public. To other readers it became evident that the subconscious (depending on who one was) can often be as interesting, not to say as lyrical, as the poet fully awake. There was also a game they often played (the results, too, were sometimes printed) which can be compared, on a high intellectual level, to the game called "Consequences." One person writes a sentence, which is then covered save the last word, and the next person writes a sentence onto it, all at random, until a complete text has been created.

La Révolution Surréaliste, produced on astonishingly little money, published a very great variety of subject-matter, and all of it—from straight Marxims and political criticism of the way the country was run, to the latest "fortuitous encounter" of all sorts of material objects that had come together "on their own" (by medium of the artists)—was somehow grouped convincingly under the term surrealism. Had there been no dada movement earlier, had there been no cubism, could all this have come into being? It needed the genius of Aragon, Breton, and Eluard, in particular, to bring it to so active and imperious a fruition. Whatever was thought about it—and numerous were its enemies who felt they were being attacked or mocked—it is undeniable that it produced some fine writings and a world of paintings, designs, montages, collages, and exotic assembled pieces. Moreover, the taste with which all of this was presented was always extremely individual and technically first-rate.

From the start of surrealism in 1925, or so, until the end of 1928, Aragon, Breton and all the rest were one united group; but a little later surrealism was at an end for Aragon and several of the others who followed him and veered away then definitely towards the political side of communism, while not at all abandoning their own writing. It is Breton, also at one time a member of the Comunist Party, who has remained to this day its inmost core and leader.

Had one to examine the entire list of foreign and last-century works that the surrealists took unto themselves, I cannot believe anything could be found at all resembling Lewis Carroll's *The Hunting of the Snark*. In its far-flung embrace of subjects and manners so disparate, surrealism has only one Snark.

Snark was Aragon's suddenly voiced choice, and I cannot remember if anything in particular led to it. But I do remember thinking that even he, with his literary adroitness and good English, would find it impossible to translate. That he can juggle the French language like the virtuoso he is is known to all who read him. But consider the entity of the thing. Is it not purely English humor? How can the spirit of it go into another language? I wondered. And, then, it is so much of its time. "Ah, there you are wrong," said Aragon. "*Le Snark* is of all time, it cannot be dated. You'll see what I shall make of this translation; I can hear it already in my head."

It was astonishing to see the ease and speed with which he put *Snark* into French, amidst all the confusion of carpenters and electricians still at work in Le Puits Carré. I see him yet, forging ahead, with a smile on his fine lips and a growing sheaf of papers, sitting on this step or that, with a pencil and an old copy of *Snark*. To him it became a terrestrial daily companion for four or five days, so rapid was he at putting it into French.

He admired the two Alices greatly, but the *Snark* was entirely to his purpose. Someone French might ask: "What is it—a political satire?" No, just its own surging, unclassifiable self. These strange figures, motivated by no one can tell what springs, wandering about uncharted seas on a craft now led, now driven, were ideal to Aragon "at this time of day"—which may sound a rather political phrase, but I mean only that the strange vagary suited his mood.

What would Lewis Carroll have thought of his translator? Aragon swore that he would have understood surrealism; here was the very proof of it, in his writings! The Wonderland, Looking-Glass worlds, too, were within the orbit of the supra-natural. That the translator should have been the man he was might have surprised Carroll—the intense, slight, sometimes violent, and very charming Aragon, then thirty-one years old, whose last two volumes of poems at the time (*Le Mouvement Perpétuel* and *La Grande Gaité*) expressed so much love, passion, exultation, tragedy, sarcasm, even despair; they were, in fact, the revolutionary surge of a fiery temperament that was its own law and way of being.

Aragon was a demon for work and seldom seemed tired. Having put *Snark* into French so felicitously he was eager to see what it would look like in proof, and together we set up a few lines. His hands were deft, the printing-stick seemed as if already known to him, and the critical moment of emptying the *composteur's* five lines onto the tray passed without mishap. And even setting the four made-up type-pages in correct juxtaposition for the sheet laid atop for printing in a way that correct pagination would ensue, seemed not too difficult. To me this was almost a nightmare, but Aragon had a host of ideas and was rapid, careful, and creative.

Composing however took a rather long time. It is extraordinary what a difference there is between reading a work the length of the *Snark* and setting and printing it by hand. If one does a full page each day, a page of my large format which took in five or six verses, that is a very fair average. And there were extras, such as the little decorative strip at the top of each page, composed in "Snark" letters, and the map, the preface, and the printing of the front cover. This cover is one of my most striking, and quite unlike any other book cover I have ever seen.

All of this and our buoyant spirits seemed odd to M. Lévy, and rather disconcerting. Beginners should not behave this way. He could not make us out. My being English, I suppose, accounted for anything incomprehensible to him on my score. But Aragon, a fellow Frenchman! He never dared ask Aragon directly the meaning of *Le Surréalisme*. In any case, there was soon a passage of *Snark* which might be taken as a sample. Was *this* it? He shook his head, but not too perceptibly. The French of it was, of course, impeccable, so it could not be dismissed as doggerel. But the story, the theme, the characters in this weird piece? *"C'est un animal fabuleux"* ended by silencing him. But, he seemed to think, is it worth printing? Was not the ocean map, with its mere North, South, East, West indications, singularly uncommunicative? To tell him that the *Snark* was a long-consecrated British classic could not but have reinforced his opinion of the vagaries of *la perfide Albion*. No, we were certainly not mutually inspiring, or even comfortable fellow-workers, he and I. Yet work well together we did, for he was a good and careful printer and my esteem for the professional side of him increased.

One day an amusing incident occurred that must have made M. Lévy decide to be just the printer and stop offering opinions on surrealism. As I have said, visitors at Réanville were rare, but one afternoon, quite unexpectedly, Susan Breton, the wife of the surrealist artist André, and André Masson came to see us. Their pleasure and amusement at finding Aragon and me at work was such that the printery rang with jokes and laughter. When they had left, M. Lévy came to the charge while I was alone.

"So *that's it*, is it! That's a surréaliste! *Mais quelle é-va-po-rée!*" He had spoken his piece. Nothing remained to be said.

I greatly admired Aragon's interest and absorption in whatever he was doing, and his innate competence. To me it is no surprise that, despite the myriad warring problems and complications, he has kept ever to the straight line chosen by him a little later that same year. He was not yet a member of the French Communist

Party, but became one in Paris soon after leaving the Hours and Réanville. To my mind, the poet and creative writer remain in him supreme. Politics have not ousted either and it is good to remember this, faced with those who hold that a creative artist will probably lose himself on account of so thoroughly embracing a political belief and party— "especially *that* party," many will add.

That energy of his, that quickness of brain and deftness of hand. On one occasion he successfully defied many of the technical difficulties that exist perforce in a medium new to one, as was printing to him. He had been *aide-chirurgien* in the 1914–18 war, and maybe this partly explained the firm yet delicate touch of his hands in setting type and make-up. Type, when of the same size, is one thing; the complexities that can be computed by arithmetic begin when two or more sizes have to be used. It is then that *les blancs*, the spaces, must be so carefully thought out and fitted. And the fitting in of ornaments, vignettes, and the like is about the very last thing one may be supposed to learn when one begins printing. This, however, is what Aragon set himself to do in one solitary, all-night session in the printery. Next morning, tired but triumphant, what should he bring me but three or four different versions of a design which might be used as the printed cover of *Le Snark*. The precision of these small black arabesque motifs, all perfectly set together, gave the impression of a pattern carried out in black iron lace, and one of the versions was subsequently used for the cover. M. Lévy could not get over this, for it was, indeed, an exploit in printing. Aragon had been at typesetting a mere two or three weeks and had turned out several samples of ornamental composition that would have honored any of the seven-year printers Lévy had told us of.

47

This was soon followed by another single-handed "exploit" of Aragon's, the composition of a very short poem called *Voyageur*, of which he printed only twenty-five copies for friends. It must be one of the rarest (possibly *the* rarest?) of his writings. Here, too, he had juggled with arithmetical computations and, on the cover, different sized letters.

A tragic *cri du cœur, Voyageur* can in some sort be rendered thus:

> From port to port, for ever onward faring,
> Ever more sad became the traveller.

The word in French is not "port" but a feminine word connected with love. And yet, "port," I think, can convey a sense of the thought. There was no need to show this item to M. Lévy.

For the translation Carroll could have had nothing but praise, so smooth and so close is it to the original, so exact and full of guileless ease. I think he would have been astonished at the way these mid-Victorian characters could suddenly be seen as men without nation, the one transposed into a "*vieux loup de mer*," the Beaver become "*le gentil Castor occupé avec sa dentelle.*" But then, it might be said, do not all those who cruise the seas develop a sort of supra-national identity?

The opening lines convey Aragon's skill:

> L'endroit rêvé pour un Snark cria l'Homme à la Cloche
> Qui débarquait l'équipage avec soin
> Soutenant chaque homme à la crête des vagues
> Par un doigt pris dans ses cheveux.

48

Just the place for a Snark! the Bellman cried,
As he landed his crew with care;
Supporting each man on the top of the tide
By a finger entwined in his hair.

But his ability to translate what seemed to me untranslatable, while retaining the spirit and sense of the original, is illustrated in this stanza:

Il répondait à Hep ou à n'importe quel cri vulgaire
Comme Mes-puces ou Mes-bottes
A Comment-que-tu l'appelles ou à Au-diable-son-nom
Mais spécialement à Trucmuche.

He would answer to "Hi!" or to any loud cry,
Such as "Fry me!" or "Fritter my wig!"
To "What-you-may-call-um!" or "What-was-his-name!"
But especially "Thing-um-a-jig!"

To me, love it as I do, *Snark* remains a kind of moon-literature. The critic of the *Times Literary Supplement* felt differently however. Acclaiming Aragon's translation as a "masterpiece in its way" and complimenting the poet for his "rhymeless and rhythmic line" which reproduced the cadence of the original, he concluded that, if one could omit Carroll's mythology, "the *Snark* in Mr. Aragon's French reads like a metaphysical poem of the modern school."

Lewis Carroll (how I should have liked his opinion at finding himself now in the surrealist domain) had been dead over fifty years, so that no copyright permission had to be obtained before the translation could appear.

Henry Crowder, who had helped in many different ways already, was familiar with *Alice in Wonderland*, and now, on first reading the *Snark*, "thought very highly of it." Together we folded the sheets into pages as they came off the new Minerva press I had just bought to increase the tempo of our work. This operation saved time at the binders in Paris. When the more than 300 bound volumes in their scarlet, black-lettered covers returned, we packed all that were sold and sent them off registered. The more expensive copies on Japan paper sold at once, and a very good number of the regular edition. Sales were excellent in France, but rather moderate in England. This registering was done on the advice of Norman Douglas, who pointed out that all works at such prices deserved "to be protected as much as possible from the foreign postal services." Not one was ever lost.

Richard Aldington

The Eaten Heart

To reread certain works after they have lain for years in memory surrounded by admiration is sometimes to discover something as fresh and beautiful as at first reading. And this (although I had reread it several times after publication), is the case with Richard Aldington's long romantic, philosophical poem *The Eaten Heart*. The same balanced measure and pace are here: all is as I remember it in its own time, the spring of 1929. This is much to the good, for often the tempo of work will appear to have changed during the passage of several years; or the development of the poem, remember it as well as one may, may no longer seem the same. One proof of its excellence surely lies in the fact that it is as moving as when Aldington first gave it me to print.

I knew it almost by heart at the end of setting it myself, in the first days of that hard-come spring, with its sharp, cold sunsets that marked not the end of my day in the printery. Music came wafting from the house, for Henry studied hard at the piano. The poem was most agreeable to set and M. Lévy became actually laudatory about the look of my pages. An intimate communion with a long, intense poem, is already there, if one reads it as often as one does, say, *The Waste Land*. How much more so when, letter by letter and line by line, it rises from your fingers around the type.

I had first met Aldington in Rome, in October 1928, after a party at Ezra Pound's apartment. To me he looked the typical Englishman, and not the type I find particularly comely. His hair was cider-red, his cheeks rosy, not large, and he was shy and arrogant at the same time. I remember we had a delightful afternoon in Rome, or rather in the strikingly beautiful Roman countryside, in carriage. How interested he was in my Hours Press, and how full of queries and suggestions. We suddenly both thought of Ezra. Had he recovered from the previous evening? We would investigate at once. Calling at his place we found him, prone, with Dorothy Pound hovering nearby. Ezra chatted, but he had soon to be left alone.

I went on to Venice before returning to Réanville, reading in my cramped *couchette* Orioli's just published edition of Lawrence's *Lady Chatterley's Lover*.

It was not until one weekend in Paris in November that I met Aldington again. Afterwards, there was much correspondence with him, and no one could have been friendlier at that time and more full of ideas for the Hours than he. Had it been a larger concern, no doubt several of his ideas could have materialized; they were all for increasing work and development. He too, I think, could not know how lengthy work is on hand presses, and I say again that this has to be experienced to be properly understood. In him, then, was a generosity of spirit, and it was largely due to him that James Hanley was able to break out of the rut of crippling poverty and show his merit. I remember Aldington's enthusiasm over a short story sent him by this earnest new writer, and his exclamations and letters to me about how much Hanley deserved to be helped, with money for a typewriter, and also literary encouragement. He took the matter in hand himself and soon Hanley became known.

At this time Aldington was living in France and had spent some time with D. H. Lawrence in the South during the latter part of the writer's illness. If only some of his letters to me could have survived. These would show how deeply he felt about him and how upset he was at the thought of his coming death. There was much about Lawrence in those many letters that are all gone, thanks to the war.

He was apparently one of those who, while able to delight in the vivid life of Paris in those days, shook his head angrily over the future. Bitter within himself (though not very visibly so to me) on account of the horrible experiences he had been through, he was gay in company, and many a good evening went by when Ezra Pound, Walter and Lillian Lowenfels, Louise Theis, Henry Crowder, Bridget Patmore, Aldington, and I met in Paris. To see Richard and Henry laughing together, to hear them talk about America, especially about the ironies of the race and color question, was very worth while. There was something serenely static about Henry's way of putting things, and his eloquent descriptions were often drawn out by Aldington, who appreciated as much as I whatever it was that made Henry so buoyant. Loathing all those racial injustices as he did, there was something of a "shrug it off" attitude to him "since it won't be mended for a long time," although naturally he was never ready to countenance an affront. Such things never came up while we were all together in this or that Paris café or cabaret. I used to think of Aldington then as one born to enjoy a happy rather than an unhappy nature, but when the conversation took a serious turn he was bitter indeed, and introspective, though never so in the heavily psycho-analytical manner of the Central European intellectuals, of whom I knew many.

My edition of *The Eaten Heart* came out about a year and a half before his greatly acclaimed war novel, *Death of a Hero* appeared. All went very smoothly with the production of *The Eaten Heart*, which was printed on handsome Haut Vidalon paper on the Mathieu press, which responded as well as with *St. George* to the in-octavo jésus format. All went well, that is, until binding day. And that day we might have been killed together, Henry and I. We were driving to a new binders in nearby Evreux, with the car full of the folded sheets of *Eaten Heart*, when another car crashed into us head on. No one was hurt except me, however only slightly, but both cars were damaged. And this disagreeable experience had a horrible aftermath in the courts of Evreux a month later, where amid the dire sentences passed on some poachers and a few, sad vagrants by three irate magistrates, Henry was condemned to a month's imprisonment and 1,000 francs fine. Luckily, as it was considered a first offence, the fine was all that came of it. But Henry and I were aroused to hatred for the type of Frenchmen who seize the opportunity of coming down hard on a foreigner, and Aldington had many a stinging thing to say about this too.

The Eaten Heart is a noble, bitter, and tragic poem, partly philosophical, partly romantic, inspired by an ancient tale of love and death. The introduction recounts the medieval legend on which it is based. It says that Margarida, the wife of King Raimon of Roussillon, was greatly loved by the noble Guilhem de Cabestans and that she returned his love. Discovering this, the king had him

54

THE HOURS PRESS

CHAPELLE-RÉANVILLE EURE FRANCE

THE FIRST VOLUME, SET UP AND PRINTED BY HAND, ISSUED
FROM THIS PRESS WILL BE

PERONNIK THE FOOL   *by GEORGE MOORE*
Revised Edition of 200, each copy numbered and signed by the
author. - PRICE 2 GUINEAS -   *Ready at Christmas.*

ST GEORGE AT SILENE   *by ALVARO GUEVARA*
A Poem. With cover design by the author. Edition of 150, each
copy numbered and signed by the author. - PRICE 10 SHILLINGS
AND 6 PENCE -   *Ready in the New-Year.*

THE HUNTING OF THE SNARK   *by LEWIS CARROLL*
The first Translation into French.   •

LA CHASSE AU SNARK   *par ARAGON*
An Edition of 200 numbered copies signed by the translator.
- PRICE 1 GUINEA - 125 FRANCS -   *Ready in the New-Year.*

THE EATEN HEART   *by RICHARD ALDINGTON*
A Poem. Edition of 250, each copy numbered and signed by the
author. - PRICE 1 GUINEA -   *Ready about Easter.*

THE PROBABLE MUSIC OF BEOWULF *by EZRA POUND*
A Conjecture - Edition of 150, with a reproduction of the music.
Each copy numbered and signed by the author. - PRICE 10 SHILLINGS
AND 6 PENCE -   *Ready in the early spring.*

ONE DAY   *by NORMAN DOUGLAS*
A limited Edition, and a special Edition of 200 on hand-made
paper numbered and signed by the author.

A CANTO   *by EZRA POUND*
Limited Edition. Each copy numbered and signed by the author.
        As soon as ready.

A PLAQUETTE OF POEMS   *by IRIS TREE*
Limited Edition, each copy numbered and signed by the author.

The Hours Press list of forthcoming books

slain and ordered his heart to be made into an exquisite dish of which he bade Margarida partake. When to his question she replied that she had relished it, Raimon held up the bloody head of her lover, whose heart she had just eaten. Seeing this, she cried, "That which you gave me to eat was so good that no other food or drink shall ever pass my lips"; and cast herself to death from the high battlement. Later the lovers were avenged by King Anfos of Aragon, who made war on Raimon and had Margarida and Guilhem buried together in the Cathedral of Perpignan.

The tale serves as Aldington's comment on the love-sorrow that is found in the life of man within the loneliness of his own soul. Early in the poem, Philoctetes, coming from "a ten years prison," grasps the hand of Neoptolemus, expecting thereby to end his loneliness, but finds instead that there is no deliverance from solitude. Modern man confronts a similar fate: release from self and solitude can never occur since no one can respond to his wish to communicate. So the "one thing worth achieving"— release from self, escape from the awful loneliness—is unobtainable. And even for those who, like the lovers in the Provence tale who find release and response, whose natures do combine, the end is death, their fate "the last variety of this tragedy." Hence even they at last know Philoctetes' fate too.

The binding of *The Eaten Heart* was better in idea than in execution, for the gold lettering of the title did not stamp well on to the dark green marble paper boards. But sales were steady and excellent, and I remember good reviews, such as this one from the *Morning Post*: "This profound poem on the true significance of true love is a worthy sequel and supplement to Donne's 'Ecstasy' and the poems on the same theme by Meredith, Coventry Patmore and Lascelles Abercrombie. It well deserves the fine format of the limited edition in which it appears."

Norman Douglas

One Day

Throughout the twenty-nine years we knew each other (at times extremely well as when travelling together in Tunisia in1938, and then in London during the second half of World War II), to me Norman Douglas was the complete meaning of "a grand man"—strong in character, lively, generous, creative, witty, honest, a forceful personality as much objective as subjective, an enchanting companion—and a magnificent writer. So my book of memories of him is simply called *Grand Man*.

I met Norman first in Florence with the Sitwells in 1923 and then, later, on Capri with the writer Bryher. For awhile we did not see each other enough for friendship to develop. But there were several other meetings in Italy soon after, which showed how quickly we could become great friends. Yet it was with slight trepidation I went to stay with him in his apartment in Florence, on the Lungarno delle Grazie, in October, 1928, not long after I had printed for him the copies of his *Report on the Pumice-Stone Industry of the Lipari Islands*.

By now he was known as "Uncle Norman" to a good many people. Among them Harold Acton and Victor Cunard, both of whom, then living in Italy, knew him delightfully well. To them he was a friend and a mentor;

but the aureole of his fame made me at this time a little shy of him. Yet how absurd. By the first evening the shyness was gone forever, for he was spontaneity itself, and all differences of age and of occupation, when together, seemed inexistent. His alert mind was enchanting, and so was his interest in all kinds of small, daily things, and his determined casting out of tiresomely conventional values. He came to one, as it were, with a whole train of sympathetic qualities, of glad surprises and of good counsel. His spontaneity was most human. He would never talk of fascism to me, which was a pity, for I could imagine the trenchant kind of details he would know about it, having seen all of its evolution. It was abruptly dismissed, although one perceived how much he detested what it stood for. He had absorbed all the art side of Florence years before which was sufficient to his needs, and he joked a good deal about what appeared to him the exaggerated art-shop that operated there.

In 1928 he was beautifully afloat on the successful current of the *Lungarno Editions* where, thanks to the founder of this publishing house, his dearest friend, the delightful Pino Orioli, he had begun some years before to produce his own works. This meant that he was his own publisher from start to finish, in private editions, and well indeed he managed to make them pay. Between 1925 and 1930, Norman had published, either at Orioli's or elsewhere, ten works: *Experiments; Birds and Beasts of the Greek Anthology; In the Beginning; Some Limericks; Nerinda,* which Norman dedicated to me; *How about Europe?; Paneros; Capri—Materials for a Description of the Island;* and, of course, *Report on the Pumice Stone Industry,* which I had done at Hours, and *One Day,* which Norman gave me to do during this visit.

Already very famous, appreciated, and collected as a stylist and creative writer, he showed me while I stayed with him how much profit could be made out of hard work with good writing for a start, paid for at what he called "reasonable prices at last!" He had turned himself into a one-man printer, supervisor, accountant, publisher, and packer. String and paper were ever near in the right quantity, and the crackle of his voice is with me yet: "Mind you, never forget to register everything!" At this moment I take down Norman's *How about Europe?* from the shelf and find in it inscribed, "*68* parcels off this morning, November 23, 1929."

Swift, methodical, precise, he was up very early each morning despite the generally long evening with Orioli in some *trattoria*, and then prolonged with local wines and good conversation till a late hour in his or Pino's apartment. Handfuls, armfuls of correspondence would be collected daily at Cooks after a first visit, perhaps, to the printers. Then came a good, long lunch together, the two of us, while he laughed at me for going to see even more of "those preposterous frescoes." Then would come a confabulation with Orioli and probably another visit to the works, where he said not one of the printers knew a word of English—a serious matter to those engaged in producing books in that language. Packing and posting and correspondence followed; it was a full day. That is how I found Douglas that October, just as Lawrence's *Lady Chatterley's Lover* was being brought out privately by Orioli. I can still see Douglas snorting his contempt for the book as he tackled some unwieldy looking beginning of a parcel, and the deftness of his hands as, cracking some joke at me, he cut the string with a testy gesture, exclaiming, "To hell with all this!" It was all as expert as could be.

These Were the Hours

Douglas's feeling for Italy was great and his knowledge of it extensive, as his *Siren Land, Old Calabria,* and *Alone* show. Extensive, too, was his knowledge of classic Greek and Latin writers, and people would sometimes wonder why he had not written of Greece as well. This he himself could not explain, for of course he had travelled there at various times. No, not one book on that country.

And then, suddenly, he said that yes, after all, there was something, and that it was I who should publish this. He confided (but he has also put this into print) that he once received £300 from the Greek Government to write a book on the land, the people, and the cities—anything that took his fancy. But what had happened? Nothing had come to him in the way of inspiration, nothing. He could not for some imperceptible reason, simply could *not* write that book. Yet what he put into my hands was certainly a book about Greece; it would be fair to call it at least a good-sized fragment, if not what had been expected of himself by himself and by those who commissioned him. But there is sometimes so much personality in a work (and that is so here) that its lack of length appears inconsequential. This certainly seemed the case to me with *One Day*, as the enchanting book is called; there is so much essence in its treatment and writing that it is far from being a fragmentary composition.

This rich essay I have described in *Grand Man*:

Full and condensed, pungent and happy is this *one* day overlooking Athens, remembering several other times here, from that first one of all, at the urgent behest of his Guardian Angel who bade him leave things just as they were at that moment with Cora in England! There are enchanting snatches of talk with Greek children ("quite clever enough without going to school at all"), vignettes or sequences about Byzantine churches and artificial grottoes (most convenient for removal, twenty-two or more of them are now in the United States), and Sophocles, who was born here, and the *pentelizein* or five-stones game of old played *still* by the children amid the rocks and dust. The trees are gone, mostly, and it is hot summer, "all dust and glare," and yet it has its own charm. As for the wine, that yellow *rezzinato*, treat it like English beer, gulp it down! The third glass—it is getting on for sunset—evokes some fine thoughts on his travelling companion, *The Poets of the Greek Anthology*,

of which Douglas wrote this: "It discloses Greece from every point of view—art, philosophy, history, criticism, social life . . . Greek art has the peculiarity that it spoke both rightly and firstly. We read these lines and realize that nothing in our hearts has changed."

Blessed be the hour of sunset! He has climbed and climbed and now come, with more wine, some thoughts on the ancients: "So sensitive were they to delicate shades of feeling that these pages might well be regarded as a textbook of good manners." He begins thinking about epigrams (how interesting is this in the light of his admiration for only one kind of poetry) when he says: "They were actually hacked with an iron implement into the marble of a tomb." The only poetry Douglas admired was that of utmost conciseness, that of "the inevitable ring," as he termed it. So, after thoughts such as "the diffuseness in Pater" and "our Gothic distrust of clean thinking" night has come. Sitting on above Athens in the moonlight, now in front of good food and more wine, epigrams of his own begin coursing through his mind. How would things sound if written in some such form, he wonders—say this about the Albert Memorial: "A venerated Queen of Northern Isles reared to the memory of her loving Consort a monument whereat the nations stand aghast. Is this the reward of conjugal virtue. Ye husbands, be unfaithful . . ." Another, in the Metrodorus manner: "A ship of stout oaken timber, ploughing the broad ocean and laden with corn, arrives from Alexandria after twelve days' journey. Say, stranger, how old is the captain?" There follow other witty and beautiful epigrams: "Why always 'Not yet'? Do flowers in spring say 'Not yet'?" And then the day, this one day, is enfolded in night. Closing the book you may well find a fragrance of thyme around you.

These Were the Hours

We began work on *One Day* several months after my visit to Douglas, in May 1929, and dealing with this personal and loving tribute to Greece was very agreeable, if lengthy. It would come to some sixty pages and, yes, Monsieur Lévy was right. *Peronnik* had shown us that we had to interrupt our rhythm of work, either composing or actual printing, and distribute the type, so as to have enough for composing the next few pages. The hire of a considerable amount of monotype to be set by hand was the solution. It was fetched from Paris by Henry whose fears about transporting so much type were justified, for such a weight of lead did slightly damage the springs of the car.

I do not remember any letters from Douglas concerning the work. Proficient as he now was in book-production, he might have been writing me for samples, and certainly for proofs. But everything was left to me, and complete confidence reigned between us during the two and a half months that went into *One Day*. Its end papers are reproductions of that excellent photograph Douglas took of the Temple of Bassae, with Edward Hutton (to whom the book is dedicated) seated in the foreground, for this was at the time of the journey they took to Greece together. The two illustrations are portraits of Norman. One shows the author as a smart, young dandy, about the time he knew (and left) Cora and was a secretary in the British Embassy at St. Petersburg. The other is Douglas in much later life, with his piercing gaze, perhaps at one of those times he was striding about all over Calabria.

The binding of the signed edition of two hundred is an agreeable scarlet leather with the title stamped on the front in gold, a reproduction in Douglas's writing of the words *One Day*. The other edition of three-hundred is in dull mauve paper boards. On the whole this was the most ambitious of all my productions and it was turned out without blemish by the Paris binders.

The signed edition was priced at three guineas a copy and was almost entirely subscribed for before publication; the other likewise. And the trick played on me by one of the best-known American bookshops came to no bad end, for the returned volumes were immediately sold in England after the excellent reviews at the time of publication in July. This trick deserves to be recorded as a sample of what one may come across now and again. The order placed by the American bookshop had been for about a score of volumes, some of both editions. A few weeks later, payment came for about half; the rest were returned. A letter followed complaining that my prices were too high; although previously agreed to, of course, they were now found too high for the American buyer. But curiously enough, at the same time, through someone having sent me an American book catalogue, I was able to read with surprise that my own prices had been increased by about one third by this very shop. Transmitting the fact to Douglas was to evoke a snort of contempt and the remark that I did well in following his advice in not giving more than 10 per cent discount to the trade. There was never any hitch with English booksellers about being paid, and being paid to time.

Arthur Symons

Mes Souvenirs

Among the many writers and literary people who encouraged me in the venture of the Hours Press was Arthur Symons, who said one day that he would like me to publish something of his. Now what should it be? Something literary yet very personal, he said, and for quite a while things were left at that. We had known each other lengthily, since 1915, in the old Café Royal and Eiffel Tower restaurant days. He was constantly in both and ever full of talk with me of his life in France, knowing that I loved France and was living there in the twenties.

The very name Arthur Symons seems to evoke *The Yellow Book* and the nineties rather than any other period of his long life (he died in 1945), and I fancied he always thought of himself as a *fin de siècle* figure. It was he, in his youth, who had Verlaine to stay with him in London and welcomed him to Oxford. He was, in some sort, a kind of "ambassador" of the then contemporary French literature to England and introduced Baudelaire there. In the middle twenties his thoughts were still so much on Mallarmé that I remember letters from him saying a good translation of his poetry was necessary. Did I think I could make the attempt? Whether in his conversation with everyone he lived in such a past, I cannot tell, but he often

66

talked so interestingly of it that it is a pity no notes could have been taken of the things he said to me. Numerous were the details of how the *fin de siècle* had looked in France, and of the "vitality" of the "decadence" in England.

How his mind ran on that period. Nearly every time we saw each other he would talk of Verlaine and Rimbaud, of Baudelaire and Mallarmé, of the decadence of the nineties, and then of Whistler, Wilde, Conder, Beardsley, and Ernest Dowson, for whose poems he wrote a beautiful preface.

I waited, wondering what he was going to send me to print. It was in the summer of 1929 that *Mes Souvenirs* arrived at Réanville. In preparation for a month or more, until the end of July, it appeared neatly bound into plain biscuit-colored paper boards, with the title in gold capital letters. Sales were good. The short book of three enchanting literary essays had been expressly written for me, he said, an honor that grew the more in my eyes after reading with what freshness and personality he had written these pages on Verlaine, on "Bohemian Chelsea," and on the Indian poetess, Sarojini Chattopadhya, in "The Magic of the East."

In the days when Arthur Symons befriended George Moore, who lived at the turn of the century in the Temple in London just before moving to Dublin on behalf of the Irish Renaissance, Symons was a force to be reckoned with. His poems were held in high esteem; he was recognized as a remarkable critic. Is it the poet in him which makes most for the excellence of his essay on Verlaine? It has a poet's vision, and also the sharp outline of the best kind of visual reporting.

After saying how he met Verlaine in the company of the

French poet Charles Morice in Paris, what a picture he sets out to give of him. He had expected to meet a sort of caricature, he says, so much had the drunken, disreputable side of the great poet been publicized. But this was not so. It was in the Café François Premier on the Boulevard St. Michel that he met "this extraordinary creature whom I expected to find very much the caricature in *Hommes d'Aujourdhui, en diable,* ending in a green tail." Of Verlaine's face, Symons writes: "A strange contradictory one, with its spiritual forehead, its animal jaw, its shifting fawn's eyes. But it was genial and it had a singularly manful air; a really gentlemanly air, I might add. The eyes were certainly curious: oblique, constantly in movement, with gestures (there is no other word) of the lids and brows."

Full of vehemence, Verlaine talked to Symons of his admiration for Swinburne and Tennyson, and—of all things—of the English Sunday! He seems to have liked the English poet at sight, for he launched into anecdotes; as Symons notes, "always the most dubious ones in the most matter-of-fact and impersonal manner with the good-humoured tone of a man who simply tells a story that may interest one."

Verlaine was then living in the Hotel des Mines, 65 Boulevard St. Michel, and invited Symons to go to him next evening. But next day he had forgotten and it was by chance they met in the street, the memory of the invitation having remained at the bottom of last night's glass. A bottle of rum at two francs was sent for in the miserable bedroom, and Verlaine talked and talked about himself, searching sometimes in English for the rough French expressions he wanted to convey. He was then forty-seven, and said he was a Catholic, "mais Catholique du Moyan Age," a qualification not missed by Symons.

He expressed himself beautifully and trenchantly, and Symons reflected that all his ills (he was now at the height of his fame) came from his lack of compromise with the accepted rules of society. As he puts it: "So much licence is allowed on the one side, so much liberty foregone on the other." "Never," he adds, "was there a nature more absolutely impelled to act itself out, more absolutely alien to every conceivable convention than that of Verlaine."

Though Verlaine's face seemed to be "without a beautiful line," it was "full of character, full of somnolence and sudden fire, in which every irregularity was a kind of aid to the crayon, and could not but tempt the artist desiring at once to order a significant likeness and to have his own share in the creation of a picture." Many were those who painted and drew Verlaine: Carriere, Cazals, Anquetin, Rothenstein were among them. Of the Rothenstein work Symons writes that one feels it "could have answered Delacroix's requirement: that the artist should be able to sketch a man falling from a fourth floor window during the time it takes him to reach the ground." (What a simile to apply to that essential which is outline!) He adds: "Rothenstein, in such work as these lithographs of Verlaine and in the solemn, almost hieratic medaillon, has given us with his extraordinary vividness, less and less criticism, more and more vision. One finds in the Verlaine he has evoked, well, really a kind of actual Verlaine."

Of the mixture of good and evil in the poet he has much to say. "Passion, wisdom, creative genius, the power of mystery or colour, it has been wisely said, are allotted in the hour of birth and can neither be assimilated nor learned. For good and evil—for he was a mixture of good and evil—Verlaine possessed all these qualities. Verlaine is always faithful to himself, to the two sides of himself, and he has thus succeeded in rendering, as no one has ever before, the whole *homo duplex*, the eternal conflict of humanity."

"I imagine that in Verlaine's soul," he continues, "there was never any conscious distinction between reality and imagination, between what to most people is the prose and poetry of actual existence. His whole nature, otherwise perhaps useless enough, was always waiting to turn to poetry. No such temperament has been since Villon, and not in the least because both in Villon and Verlaine were picturesque vices to attract attention, and because both fell in with the scum and lees of society. What in Verlaine became soiled with evil might, under other chances and influences, have made part of the beauty of a Saint Francis. He had an inconceivable simplicity of nature, and those profound instincts which are really the instincts of the gentleman. Whenever he was not under the influence of those drinks which were offered him all day long by the people who called themselves his friends, he was the most delightful companion. His queer, rambling, confidential talk, full of wonder, trouble, and gaiety, was always on the verge of poetry, which in him was hardly more than the choice and condemnation of a mood or a moment. All his verse is a confession of what was beautiful and dreadful and merely troublesome to him in life, at first under courtly disguises, and then, gradually, with more and more sincerity to fact as well as to emotion or sensation, and at the end, in a pitiful enough way, a sort of nakedness in rags."

I quote at such length because of the interest there is in this first-hand description of a great figure in poetry, and also because it seems to me such an honor that Symons should have written so well of Verlaine for me to publish his pages.

Declaring that he knows more about Bohemia itself than modern Bohemian Chelsea, Symons offers in his second essay tiny vignettes of Conder, Wilde, and several young women of Chelsea. Conder's Fancy Dress Ball at his house at 91 Cheyne Walk, in 1900, represented Chelsea at its most exotic. To it came Augustus John, "dressed like a *Débardeur* of Gavarni—the born Bohemian and the born wanderer"; Condor himself invented "the costume of a dandy of 1830, that of Balzac's Eugène de Rastignac, with white ruffles and a Parisian top-hat." The Baronne de Meyer as Iago looked "as supreme in evil as Dante's Farinala." Symons "wore a kind of Venetian domino," and his wife "wore a dress designed . . . after *The Peacock Skirt* of Beardsley, with all the flaunting colours of the actual peacock."

Symons first met Wilde in 1894 and thereafter went often to his house at 16 Tite Street. At that time Wilde "was more than ever reckless, insolent, too certain of himself; he was shadowed and tracked by that evil reputation which had grown, not suddenly, but like a growth of mushrooms."

But the "Chelsea girls" held a special fascination for Symons. First, there was Jenny ("that was not her name: I invented it after Rossetti's"), who was to be seen, often alone, sitting in the Café Royal or Eiffel Tower. Occasionally she would disappear abroad. "She had always a curious fascination of an evil kind; and with that a kind of diabolical beauty which could become, as she became, exasperating. At times, she reminded one of *La Scorpione* in Cladel's novel, with her clear profile, her nervous dark inexorable eyes; with something in her regard that was infernal." Then there were Kitty, "who changed from good to bad in a most unconventional fashion, one never knows why"; Helen, "who began by looking exotic and wearing coloured and barbaric dresses and then became less interesting"; Julia, "who reminded me of the depraved little ballet-girl in *La Femme-Enfant* of Catulle Mendès"; Liliane, whose virginal innocence of face is but the flower of a soul in which vice had sprung"; and Carmen, "who confessed to her Irish and Spanish blood, who was never quiet, who was stirred by her violent emotions, swayed by her wilder passions; she was feverish and feline."

In "The Magic of the East," the third essay, the Indian poetess Sarojini Chattopadhya (although so young she became Symons' confidante in matters of the heart), gives him a delicious description of the gypsies of India.

I never knew Symons very well, but our friendship lasted many years. The quick, nervous way he had of expressing himself, his frequent use of what might be called *fin de siècle* words, such as "daemonic," "exotic," "satanic," "macabre," when talking of this or that character of last century (and sometimes of this) are unforgotten. In those days there was still real absinthe in the Café Royal; it seemed to thrill him to find here that *sorcière aux yeux glauques* that had been the undoing of so many a soul in France. He actually looked as I imagined the intellectual of the nineties to have looked, often wearing a long Inverness cape, with a wide-brimmed, high black felt hat. And it was the same when, in 1926, he brought that most sympathetic and serene of great men, Havelock Ellis, to dinner in my apartment on the Ile St. Louis in Paris. The same again when he accompanied Iris Tree and myself to a fancy dress ball at the Opera. Although he wore ordinary clothes, I remember how much in the picture he looked, and how full of excitement and pleasure he was at the sight of a passing, reconstructed bustle.

15 Rue Guenégaud, Paris

To be able to look back on the early printing days, after a mere eight to ten months, seemed wonderful. Work had been so hard and concentrated that much time at printing seemed to have passed. At the end of the first eight months, the Hours Press was already well known in England, and also a little in the United States and France. But good as well as bad things had accrued fast. The first was the co-operation of the bookshops and their speedy payments; the same was true of individual buyers. The press had prospered in its first eight months of existence, and I rejoiced to find that I had at least doubled my capital besides having acquired and produced new stock. *Peronnick, The Eaten Heart,* and *One Day* had all sold well, and *Mes Souvenirs* was in heavy demand too. The bad consisted of the difficulties of working in the country, for a press is always needing something new. Letters are lacking for this or that; the binders become recalcitrant and want to do things their own way; and naturally, they have to be argued with in person, and convinced; they fail one in point of time. In addition, there were the frustrating delays in the mail and the sudden interruptions of the electricity. Little by little towards the end of 1929, I saw that the press would do better yet if moved to Paris, and here too I was lucky in finding not only a place to install it but for a time a fine co-worker.

It was my good friend Georges Sadoul, now so well known as the historian of the cinema, who in the winter of 1929 found a small shop with an *arrière boutique* that had just become vacant at 15 Rue Guenégaud, a narrow side street on the Left Bank near Rue de Seine and Rue Mazarine. The move to Paris in the mid-winter of 1929 was accomplished without difficulty, thanks to Sadoul and André Thirion, who helped look after this in a business-like way. The rent at 15 Rue Guenégaud was most reasonable and the rearrangement and redecorating went with ease. To think of such things nowadays seems almost fabulous. Where now are the small shops at low rents in Paris? Both are things that belong to the past.

In Paris the press began to function again at once, at irregular but productive hours with Sadoul as a rather elastic secretary and general factotum. He was then one of the most productive writers of the surrealist group, but, being in need of a small job, he worked for me many months at the Rue Guenégaud. We both knew that strictly regular hours are no *sine qua non* if one is rather bohemian by temperament. When one is one's own master and sees eye to eye with a fellow worker, then a maximum, even, can be achieved by working at all sorts of irregular hours by day or night, and this we experienced many a time. Clerking, accounts, packing, and posting were often handled by him, and the speed with which—talking of further plans for the press and the Galerie Surréaliste—his nervous fingers would unconsciously make hay out of all the objects on the surface of the Buhl table is unforgotten, and we laugh at it yet. But his rapidity in the posting of several dozen packages of books, registered all at one go, of course, is likewise remembered. He was an admirable fellow worker.

In the front of the place was a small shop, its walls garnished with books already produced, and on display a few modern abstract paintings, particularly by Miró, Malkine, and Tanguy, painted shields, fetish figures and sculptures from Africa, New Guinea, and the South Seas stood on top of the long line of bookshelves done in a neutral grey, which stood against the lighter walls. The floor was in large squares of black and white linoleum, with a beautiful Buhl writing-desk as the office table. Good lighting shone on the rich assembly of bright African beading here and there and the multi-coloured splendour of Brazilian tribal head-dresses in parrot feathers. The little place could be brought to a blaze.

In the back part stood the two presses and other working furniture. Monsieur Lévy had now left me, to our mutual consent, and there was a sympathetic, progressive-minded young printer who came and did his eight-hour day, the rhythm of the Minerva pedal press sounding pleasantly near while one talked to those who came to the shop. And yet I was also mindful that this was not an art gallery but a press where I, too, should be at work—typesetting.

At times, when the interruptions became too numerous, I took to locking the shop door onto the street; friends, however, knew of the side entrance. In all, not so very many people came there. It was in the small neighboring cafés we met, even at the *marchand de vins et charbons* almost next door— where one had a glass of red wine for about 4*d.*—and the Café de Flore and Deux Magots, which then, as now, were the literary-artistic centers on the Left Bank.

The new printery was close to the Galerie Surréaliste in

Exterior of the Hours Press, Paris

the Rue Jacques Callot, which the surrealists had started with almost no capital a year or so earlier, and which had already become the mecca of *avant-gardisme*, without exception, *the* mecca. Its character and prestige grew apace as the exhibitions of works by Picasso, Picabia, Arp, Chirico, Klee, Miró, Dali, Tanguy, Masson, Gris, Man Ray, and a score more succeeded each other. There was considerable *brio* to this gallery. It became very well known and was a center to which, besides compatriots, came many an artist and collector from abroad. Among the most recent acquisitions of their group were sculptures and carvings of the primitive peoples, then generally less appreciated than they are now. In those days, ethnography was for specialists and but few others, although some artists had seen the beauty in the "works of the savages." It was Matisse who first bought, for almost nothing, a great painted Congo mask from a village café on the banks of the Seine—so the story goes—in 1909 or so, and this event has been quoted many a time as the entry of primitive art into the realm of advanced modern painting. Before then, it was usually referred to as "objets des colonies," or "the stuff the sailors bring back," or "native curios." Such carvings and sculptures from Africa, New Guinea, and Oceania, and work by the American Indians before the time of Columbus, were on sale at the gallery at the same time as the so moderately priced pictures (now worth how many times more than their 1930 prices); many were bought by collectors from various parts of the world.

Breton, Aragon, Eluard, and most of the other surrealists had seen the affinity—and how strange it is—between such fetich figures and carvings from Africa and Oceania and avant-garde painting; the wonderful constructions from New Britain and New Ireland in the South Seas looked particularly fine in the gallery. The taste that went into its arrangement was remarkable and the ethnographical knowledge of its animators increased all the time. Much respect is due them for having been the first to create this juxtaposition between abstract painting and the often equally abstract or geometrical designs which sprang from the minds of the pre-Columbian and other tribal artificers. Many of the surrealists have written on this theme, and it was certainly thanks to them that such a vision—accepted everywhere nowadays where modern art is understood—was first presented to the public.

Aragon and I came several times to England in the mid-twenties before the Hours Press started to rake through the curio-shops and junk-dealers of several English ports and London. Ever since Curtis Moffet, the artist and photographer, had stimulated my interest in African and Oceanic art around 1921, I had found England to be an excellent hunting ground, and some of the best New Guinea and Oceanic pieces in the gallery were bought there for very little. Sadly dirty or battered, such objects reacquired their primitive gloss once in the Galerie Surréaliste. Aragon's favorite *venue*, like mine, was Africa. Breton's love was mainly for Oceania, and Sadoul's for New Guinea.

The Paris, or second series of Hours Press books, was now entirely fore-planned (insofar as a definite program could be made without allowing for sudden extras that might come along). To announce the new books, a handsome circular was printed early in 1930 and divided into three sections: poetry, prose, and music. By then I had made arrangements to publish poems by Walter Lowenfels, Robert Graves, Laura Riding, Bob Brown, Harold Acton, Roy Campbell, and Brian Howard. Richard Aldington promised a war story, and Laura Riding a prose piece called *Four Unposted Letters to Catherine*. Henry, after some energetic coaxing by me, had agreed to set several poems to music.

Since I wished all the poetry volumes to appear in the same rather large format, I thought it would be good to have covers by contemporary artists. Yves Tanguy immediately agreed to make those for the Apollinaire poem by the American poet, Walter Lowenfels. His drawings of lunary cliffs turned out beautifully. Len Lye undertook photomontages for the covers of poems by Graves and Laura Riding, and made a third design for a short prose piece by her. Man Ray, the famous American artist and photographer and founder in New York, with Marcel Duchamp and de Zayas, of the Dadaist group there in 1917, did some remarkable photomontage covers for Henry Crowder's music book. Another of my artists, Elliott Seabrooke, dressed the volume of Harold Acton's poems so agreeably, and John Banting made two of the best covers of all for the poems of Brian Howard. Roy Campbell sent along two of his drawings which were reproduced on his volume of poems, and the covers of Bob Brown's *Words* were a pleasingly adroit typographical composition by the printer John Sibthrope.

In the same circular, opposite my list of books and authors, I wrote: "All the poetry will be hand-set and most of these volumes will be printed on a Hand Press over a hundred years old. The same format to be used (in-octavo jésus) set in 16-point Caslon old-face on Haut-Vidalon, Canson and Montgolfier paper of which this is a sample page. Lithographic, typographic, photographic paper covers on boards by contemporary artists. Each copy signed by the author." There followed a list of the books printed at Réanville, including a note that *Peronnick the Fool* was out of print, and finally a notice that the Hours Press was "also interested in Ethnography— African Art, Oceania, and the two Americas—and will always have a few specimens on show, as well as certain modern french pictures, a few english and american books and the Surrealist Series."

Looking now at the circular, I see a few items announced that were never produced, such as the poems of Iris Tree, *The Probable Music of Beowulf* by Ezra Pound, cover designs by Frank Dobson, Hilaire Hiler, and Eugene MacCown. These were listed for some future date and none of them reached me.

The Hours Press books had received good notices and reviews in British magazines and newspapers, to which I never sent out more than some dozen to fifteen copies, and the move to Paris elicited some additional favorable press comments which encouraged one to think that the press had already come to the attention of many people. Among the notices that have survived are these which appeared during the course of 1930. *The Observer* wrote: "Miss Nancy Cunard's Hours Press announces a number of new poems mainly by the modernists. All of them from this house are sure to be agreeably turned out in a large, plain format." *The Nation* called "the Hours Press an interesting experiment in printing and publishing. The books are hand-set and there is none of that fussy artiness which too often disfigures this type of production." *Everyman* spoke of Hours as "one of the most interesting of the newer small presses. Here, on a hand press over a hundred years old, Miss Cunard has for some months past been issuing exquisite limited editions of modern writers, and she has the good sense which the English private publisher so often lacks to issue her wares at a price which the ordinary book collector can well afford."

On the whole, people were discouraged from dropping in at Rue Guenégaud. This was not a shop or a gallery, I said to myself, but a printery. But there one is, in the very center of Paris, and a shop, as it was as well, can be thought of as a *siège social*. A shop is open to the public. Were its books not for sale here? Sales in this manner were few, but by now I had that very estimable Mr. Gray, the book traveller, who went the rounds of the London trade and sold the Hours Press books very well indeed. Mr. Gray, like myself, liked things done to time.

Absorbing was the work, but it had changed somewhat in character and I had less and less time for typesetting, for authors were being met and talked to, publicity organized, and the bills and accounts increased and had to be dealt with. Success was good, yet it actually vexed me at times since I would so much rather have been the artisan, type-setter, and printer, proofreader, never-ending letter writer, rather than the "Director," responsible for keeping accounts in the approved French manner, with a *chiffre d'affaires* and all the rest of commercial bureaucracy. We even had to have a monthly accountant. This man would have pleased some authors as a model of pettifogging, but he was a great trial to me.

At one time Rue Guenégaud served as a refuge for a young French student of seventeen who had escaped from tyrannizing paternal authority. The father blamed the surrealists for having put subversive ideas into his head. This very brilliant young man (as he soon turned out to be) was then haunted by despair, almost to the point of suicide. His father was head of the police of a large provincial town and had treated his son to a taste of *la panier à salade,* or black maria, wherein, surrounded by gendarmes, he was taken to prison for disobedience. He had somehow escaped and Sadoul and Thirion brought him to me for hiding. I think of him with affection and admiration; he was one of my helpers in the often intricate ways of French commerce, and later became my main collaborator in the *Negro Anthology.*

Now and again a fine Miró or Tanguy would be set in the front window, and a few of the surrealist publications were on sale there. It was thus that two copies of two rare books found their way to the press for safekeeping. They were erotic works of imaginative value and beautifully written, with illustrations of fine quality, by two surrealist authors and two surrealist painters. Who can have advised anyone of their hidden presence at the Hours? Some enemy who remained forever anonymous.

One evening I was tidying the shop and smoothing out the Oceanic Tapa bark-cloths and bringing back order into the African beading that people liked to finger so much, when there appeared a peculiarly disagreeable individual. I noted the printer in the back room had a good look at him and then put his head down and went on pulling pages faster and faster.

The man was what is known as *très correcte,* rather severe, and he appeared, I thought, a little embarrassed. He did not look like a client who could want anything in English and the only French book was Aragon's *La Chasse au Snark,* in its red alignment along one shelf.

What did I print and publish? he asked. All these, said I, indicating the various books. He took up one and then another, shaking his head. What else did I sell? Some of the paintings and drawings, or possibly some ethno-graphical pieces could be found for him, or some African beading. These pieces (and he glared at them) were actually part of the decoration of the shop. No, no, said he. And then he shot me an ugly look and said he would pay a good price. But what for? He was searching for books in French. Well, they were for . . . his waiting room. My astonishment did not prevent me from putting the *Snark* into his hands. No, no, no, not that sort of thing, said he. The *salle d'attente* is . . . er . . . in rather special taste, you see. And again the printer looked up, wiping a smile off his face and bent with redoubled vigor to his work. It was the *Snark* which infuriated the man most of all and he left clumsily and rudely forthwith.

When the door had been locked after him the printer came into the shop and burst out laughing. "Why were you so polite to that *individu*? You should have told him at once you had nothing in his line and never would have. And there you were, talking about African beads and *La Chasse au Snark!*"

"But what *is* his line? I thought he might have wanted to buy something. After all, this is a shop too. What did he mean by 'waiting room' and 'special taste'?"

"Oh, Madame," said the printer, "could you not see that man is a common detective? He hoped you would fall into his trap, although why did he come here? Through some jealousy of the neighbors perhaps, in denouncing a foreign person at work on a press, which is not a very usual thing? He was posing as the owner of a brothel. Hence the 'waiting room' and the 'special taste' in books—for people to warm up on while waiting. He wanted pornography—what else? So as to be able to arrest you for selling it!"

The erotic books were soon removed and there were no

more visitations from agents whose aim is to hunt down the authors, producers and sellers of such works, making no difference between what is erotic art and what is fifth-rate smut.

Harold Acton was often at the Rue Guenégaud, which he has described deliciously in his *Memoirs of an Aesthete*. However, Harold wrote that the Hours Press seemed to function only by fits and starts. I cannot think where he got this impression, unless it came from the fact that work did not appear to weigh heavily on us. This observation is firmly contested by me, for everything got done on time, if not in a strictly academic manner. On one of his visits to Paris Harold came to the press several times with Norman Douglas.

There was certainly the day when Douglas complained to me testily of the "horrors" of some of the surrealist paintings. He was interested in the press and liked the place, but was somewhat bewildered by the propinquity of carved totem figures and surrealist abstracts. But then Douglas could also turn his mind to such ultra-moderns as his very good friend, the American poet Walter Lowenfels, who knew better than to talk to him, however, about modern abstract poetry. It was with Douglas that I met this very sympathetic man and writer, maybe a little earlier on. At any rate it was quickly decided that his long poem, *Apollinaire*, should be the first of the new series at the Hours.

Eugene MacCown

Paintings, Drawings and Gouaches

At this time there lived and worked in Paris the young American painter, Eugene MacCown, a friend of Jean Cocteau, René Crevel, Bernard Faÿ, and of how many additional French and other intellectuals. My first meeting with Eugene came one evening at the famous restaurant, Le Boeuf sur le Toit. His boyish appearance belied the sensitive artist he was, as did his mid-western drawl, for he had been born in a praire schooner. At times his curly brown hair and short nose gave him a slightly Negroid appearance. Then, too, the almond eyes, which seemed slightly pinched at the sides, could sometimes make him look oriental. I saw much of Eugene in the 1920's, traveling with him in Amalfi, Capri, Pompeii, and Florence, where with Sachie and Osbert Sitwell we met Norman Douglas, and of whom Eugene drew a curious sketch, "more of a rendering than a likeness." He had painted a full-size portrait of me in 1923, and had made the cover designs for my long poem, *Parallax*, published by the Hogarth Press, and now, in 1930, he was about to have his first exhibition at the Galérie Léonce Rosenberg in Paris. Would not the Hours, he asked, print the catalogue?

So the catalogue, simple yet somewhat deluxe, with four full-page illustrations, in pale green paper covers, was

87

made up in February 1930 and was the first Hours production since its move to the Rue Guenégaud. It was tastefully designed and its main idea may well be unique, for Eugene asked six well-known literary men, all friends of the artist, to supply the titles, individually and separately, for each painting. In his own preface, Eugene wrote:

> The purpose of the preface to an exhibition catalogue is mysterious. Lack of space prevents any serious study; and if X, Y and Z, eminent critic or collector, writes a few ornamental paragraphs praising the quality of the pictures exposed, what of it? Intelligent opinion remains uninfluenced by such amiable log-rolling. Hence I have spared one of my friends the task of composing a flowery and perhaps insincere offering, and the public the weariness of reading it.
>
> As for titles, I have never thought of them. No preface, no titles, no catalogue—perfect! But I had rather a lively idea. I asked six of my friends to make independently of one another a list of titles that each considered appropriate. The observant may discern in these lists opinions on my work, may glimpse a flash of each man's sensibility dimly revealed through these reactions or comments.
>
> Nothing to do with Painting or Art. Only a consolation for those who may find the pictures insufficient—an embellishment . . . A catalogue, finally. And this seems to be something of a preface.
>
> I thank Clive Bell, Jean Cocteau, Norman Douglas, Bernard Faÿ, André Gide and Raymond Mortimer for their cooperation.

The results of the artist's rather "lively idea" were remarkably variegated. There were twenty-three pictures and twelve drawings and the nominators reacted variously in their choice of titles. A fine trio of heads set close to each other evoked the following titles for one of Eugene's paintings: Clive Bell, "Si Jeunesse Savait"; Jean Cocteau, "Trois Personnes Qui Sont Venues Sans Etre Invitées"; Norman Douglas, "The Happy Family"; Bernard Faÿ, "Le Présent (Figure de Pierre entre deux Réves)"; André Gide, "The Unhappy Family"; and

Eugene MacCown's portrait of Nancy Cunard, 1923

Raymond Mortimer, "Intrusion of a Dead Morality."
I will not begin to suggest what glimpses each title provides
of each man's sensibility.

To some Eugene's idea may seem rather tongue-in-
cheek, for the title of a picture may well be thought of as
part of its entity. Or, saying this, am I being too literary?
It is often claimed that a painting must stand on its own
ground and not be affected by other intellectual considerations. No levity was there in any of these paintings. On
the contrary, many of them struck one as grave and
thoughtful—figures painted with care, a slight allusion in
some to Picasso, but very individual and done from a
palette of fresh, bright tones. The work of many artists
besides MacCown showed the influence of Picasso, but
one critic found Eugene's pictures "intensely individual,"
with a cleanness of line and a delicacy of detail that
revealed "the completeness of the contemporary reaction
from Impressionist methods." The same critic even
declared that MacCown's "decorative and highly poetic
work made him one of the most promising of the newest
generation of painters."

Walter Lowenfels

Apollinaire, An Elegy

Of the many widely different friends of Norman Douglas, the American poet Walter Lowenfels was, and remains, one of the most interesting. It was a tribute to both that each could appreciate the other so well, ages and occupations being so different, and Douglas admiring the barest minimum of poetry in the output of all the ages. None of that written in contemporary times appealed to him. The fact that Lowenfels was "an ultra modern" made no difference, and I have seldom heard such enthusiasm as that voiced by him for Douglas. He had met him on his first trip to Europe in 1922; they had subsequently become great friends by correspondence, and it was Lowenfels who sold for Douglas the manuscript of *South Wind* in New York.

Giving up a commercial career, to the annoyance of his rich father, Lowenfels was one of the young generation of American writers who chose to come and live lengthily in France. This was the beginning, as he wrote me, "of my second life. My first one wound up when I quit the butter business in 1926, gave up 'an assured future,' and decided I had to learn how to write." I remember how Douglas encouraged him in this, for he thought highly of him: one should do what one wants in life, "up to the hilt."

Walter Lowenfels

In the very long "Letter" Lowenfels wrote me after reading my *Grand Man*, he reminisces evocatively about Douglas:

> Everything he did had style—his relations with people, with food—his sentiment for people, his capacity for making and keeping friends, his companionships . . . With him one shared an approach to life that made it very tasty . . . He sent me to North Africa, to the Tyrol, to the "Oktober Fest" in Munich, and to re-reading the whole of Shakespeare every five years, a habit he said he found useful.

And so Lowenfels travelled much in Europe, where two people told him something about writing. "One was the sculptor Zadkine. Sitting in a cafe on the Blvd. Raspail one evening, he advised me to eliminate the word 'must.' The other person was Norman." Douglas told him he had taken all the "buts" out of a revised edition of *Siren Land!* Were all literary advice but as concise as this.

Of an ebullient, enthusiastic nature, characterized by a zest that has never grown dim, as his recent writings and letters show, Lowenfels also had his thoughtful side, and a deep sense for humanity, with a great feeling for France and its writing. He assimilated well, was critical too, and was soon liked by various French intellectuals. Seldom have I found a more naturally hospitable, giving personality.

There were many evenings when Lowenfels, tall and handsome and romantic looking, his attractive, intelligent wife Lillian, Norman Douglas, Henry Crowder, and I would enjoy good talks together. Henry revelled in the young couple and would remark, "If only *all* white Americans were like them!" The poet had a great sympathy for the American Negroes, and it was interesting to see how the often very subtle images in his *Finale of Seem* (a volume of verse which had just come out with a preface by Humbert Wolf) were understood by several musicians of color we knew in Montmartre. To me he was an ideal American, spontaneous and buoyant, generous-spirited, gay, a friend to all the good things in life, and also a hard worker. In 1930 he had begun a multi-volume work, which has turned into *The Poem That Can't Be Stopped*, of which one section is the fairly recent *American Voices*. In the Hours Press days he was recognised as one of the avant-garde poets and, in 1932, shared the Richard Aldington prize with E. E. Cummings. Work of his was coming out at that time in Eugene Jolas's *transition* in Paris, in *The Criterion*, and *The London Mercury*.

Although later, back in the United States, he developed politically to the extent of being one of the recognised forces of the Left, he was already one of those greatly moved by the execution of Sacco and Vanzetti, and the poem that Henry Crowder set to music in the volume subsequently published by the Hours is dedicated to the memory of them, and was also reproduced with the music in my *Negro Anthology*.

In our Paris days Lillian and Walter lived in a whirl of arts and travel. He was an invigoratingly vivid talker, and the same rhythm is in his letters now. His journalism has individual style. One thinks of him not at all as a propagandist but as a poet, and the evolution of his sonneteering is remarkable. *Sonnets of Love and Liberty* resounds with hope and clash, and is at the same time a strange blend of academic form and the pulsations of this century. Recently Aragon wrote somewhere that Lowenfels seemed to belong to the Shakespearian age. That will mean because of his intensity of feeling, because of the exact, and spare, and even concentrated use of words and images.

94

At the time I published his *Apollinaire*, there was already this sense in him of "time *and* timelessness" (continuity), the strange link there is in some poets between the accidental, the unknowable, and the foreseen. There was, and is, such a sense of continuity in his poetry that what had been begun in France in, or before, 1930 was taken up again, continued, and greatly developed in the very much later and different period of 1953–58. *Some Deaths*, for instance, which contained his *Elegy on Apollinaire*, is in *The Poem That Can't Be Stopped,* along with *American Voices.* There was also his power of compassion which these two passages from *Apollinaire* convey.

> Each man to his own dead
> and grief that returns with the revolving year
> but this death is more than death
>   the earth is truly wet with rainy eyes
> the world is mourning the world's own death
> dying in its creation Apollinaire.
>
>   .   .   .   .   .
>
> You who were Provence to those who went before
> came into being again
> to be Apollinaire to us
>   showing to those who saw
>   those who see
> a way to build
>   making your going out
> a coming in
>   saying
> that death that is the act
> is a passing at the point of a possible beginning
> making anywhere a beginning

any point a possibility
saying
the world is constantly building
dying into beginning
   saying
the world is enough
and that is enough

Apollinaire, hand-set and printed on Haut-Vidalon paper, was the first of the Rue Guenégaud series of seven volumes of poetry in the same in-octavo jésus format; the covers were designed by the well-known French sur-realist painter, Yves Tanguy, who drew some high, dream-inspired cliff-scapes that suggest islands floating in space. They were printed in black on buttercup yellow paper boards, with a gold-lettered, black leather spine.

Of this book, the *Everyman* critic wrote that it was "a beautiful specimen of the work of the private presses," and complimented Lowenfels' "curiously moving lament for the death of that fantastic personality, Guillaume Apollinaire."

Robert Graves
Ten Poems More
Laura Riding
Twenty Poems Less

Ten Poems More, for three reasons, was my most successful volume of poetry. First, it is a good, short collection— just eleven poems—which sold out on, if not shortly before, publication in May 1930. Second, I was able to send Robert Graves about £80 in royalties, rejoicing in the thought that fine poems, for once, were paying their author. And third, I came upon the volume years later, in 1950 or 1951, in an exhibition of fine book production throughout the ages held at the Victoria and Albert Museum, where it was among examples chosen for their handsome binding and general taste as well as individuality.

At this time, Robert Graves was working with Laura Riding at their Seizin Press at Deya, Mallorca, with the frequent co-operation of Len Lye, the remarkable Australian artist and film-maker, who made the covers for *Ten Poems More*; they are outstanding photomontages combining stones, wire netting, and rocks in beautiful fantasy and proportion. The front and back covers are joined by a narrow spine of green leather, with the title in gold lettering. The production was excellent, for by now the Paris binders understood what was required of

them. All seven books of poetry in the second series of
the Hours were uniform in format, and are the same as
that of the earlier *Eaten Heart* by Richard Aldington.

I remember there was a good deal of correspondence
during the work of production and, although I knew
Graves very slightly at the time, his letters always contained much individual considerations. Indeed they
would be interesting to read today once more, but all
disappeared during the last war so destructive of Hours
Press papers and documents. Undoubtedly one of the
most striking personalities of our time, he was not less so,
if differently, when I met him in London in 1929 than
when last seen in 1959, once again installed on Mallorca,
where he looked singularly like one's general idea of a
handsome, if benevolent, Roman Emperor. In his youth
the impression he produced on me was most peculiar.
I thought of him as a being all in nerve, and there was
something to him that suggested an equine nobility, that
evoked a strong, wilful young horse—and a wild one at
that. But then, to return to the human, there was also the
deep, thoughtful strain visible as well. On Mallorca,
I looked for all this, but the Roman Emperor was dominant
and a youthful sort of patriarchalism; maybe that arose
from his mode of life and surroundings. And there was
that easy, generous way of receiving one; Graves appeared
almost to be holding court and yet was (and is) ever very
hard at work—urbane, kindly, a beautiful talker.

Robert Graves has always been one of the best contemporary poets. His lines in this volume of seventeen
pages, despite their subtlety, have a "look you in the eye"
quality and their excellence, the ring of them, comes
with a directness of impact. Take, for example, "Oak,
Poplar, Pine" and "Act V, Scene V":

Robert Graves, Laura Riding

OAK, POPLAR, PINE

The temple priests though using but one sign
For TREE, distinguish poplar, oak and pine:
Oak, short and spreading—poplar, tall and thin—
Pine, tall, bunched at the top and well inked in.
Therefore in priestly thought all various trees
Must be enrolled, in kind, as one of these.
The fir, the cedar and the deodar
Are pines, so too the desert palm-trees are;
Aspens and birches are of poplar folk
But chestnut, damson, elm and fig are oak.
All might be simple, did the priests allow
That apple-blossom dresses the oak bough,
That dates are pine-cones; but they will not so,
Well taught how pine and oak and poplar grow:
In every temple-court, for all to see
Flourishes one example of each tree
In tricunx. Your high-priest would laugh to think
Of oak-boughs blossoming in pagan pink,
Or numerous cones, hung from a single spine,
Sticky yet sweeter than the fruit of vine,
(For vine's no tree; vine is a creeping thing,
Cousin to snake, that with its juice can sting).
Confront your priest with evident apple-blossom;
With faith and doubt, conflicting, heave his bosom?
Force dates between his lips, will he forget
That there's no date-palm in the alphabet?
Turn apostate? Even in secret? No,
He'll see the blossom as mere mistletoe.
The dates will be as grapes, good for his needs:
He'll swallow down their stones like little seeds.
And here's no lie, no hypocritic sham:

99

Believe him earnest-minded as I am.
His script has less, and mine more, characters
Than stand in use with lexicographers.
They end with palm, I see and use the sign
For tree that is to palm as palm to pine,
As apple-bough to oak-bough in the spring:
It is no secrecy but a long looking.

Act V, Scene V

"You choose the old nurse and the little page
To act survivors on your tragic stage,
Each an unnecessary player."
"No, not unnecessary", you say; "if none
Survive to moralise on what's been done
This is no tragedy but dead men's laughter.
Tears are the purge—the nurses broken line
"O mistress, pretty one, dead!" the page's whine
"Thou too? Alas, fond master!"
"No purge for my complaint: I'd have them own
Small sorrow to be left on-stage alone
And in the bloodiest royal massacre
Either rant out the anti-climax well:
"'A's dead, the bitch!" "So's Oscar; sung in Hell!"—
Then fall to rifling pocket, belt and purse
With corky jokes in character,
Or drive the feud yet further; page with nurse
His jewelled dirk against her sooty cleaver."

Most of the reviews of *Ten Poems More* are gone, but
the *Observer* critic wrote that Graves "is never easy and
he is often teasingly difficult; but the teasing is attractive,
and the obscurity is very far indeed from being pompous

Nancy Cunard with her Hours Press books, Spring 1930

or proverbial. He seizes the attention and compels a following. The squib fired at old tragedy called 'Act V, Scene V' detonates finely, and 'History of the World' puts the universe in fourteen lines. Mr. Graves, giving words scantily, never wastes them. He has at his command that compression of thought, phrase and fancy so happily wrought by the metaphysical poets of the 17th century."

Twenty Poems Less, by Laura Riding, was the companion volume to Graves's *Ten Poems More*, which it immediately followed. The title evoked a certain surprise; what was its meaning? Apart from the allusion to Graves's title (the two poets were working closely together at this time), another poet said it suggested, "Here, with these twenty poems I now give are twenty less within me." They are subtle and were to many readers somewhat difficult, one of whom was the reviewer for the *Times Literary Supplement*, who insensitively dismissed *Ten Poems More* and *Twenty Poems Less* as exercises in combining "wildly dissimilar thoughts by the frailest possible bridge of association." In a letter published in the *Times*, Laura Riding and Graves retaliated by accusing him of "defining modern poetry in terms of his own irritation with it." Fettered by traditionalism, he becomes "querulous at the idea of having to read poems with close attention rather than just splashing about in their suggestive spray." So unfit a critic has no business commenting on modern poetry. "Poetry, Sir, is reputed to be the most important of all literary classifications; and books of poems by professional poets should be handled with at least as much expertness as treatises by professional mathematicians."

After several readings, Laura Riding's poems grew on me; they were, somehow, "other world," which is a loose, groping way of answering one's own question: "What do I feel about them?" And it was in some way connected with the impression I had of her the only time I saw her, with Robert Graves, when we met in London in 1929. Distinctly supernatural? Is that what she is? I asked myself. No, indistinctly, vaguely so. Her personality was very tense, dominating, and quietly American. Like a brooding, sultry day, there was electricity around, if not visible; a sense of contained conflict. And there was, on the one hand, the terrific, clinical tidiness of everything in the London flat—a hand press I remember in particular, with its accessories about it in a way no printer would take time off to keep so clean, almost as if in a museum. On the other hand, there was an eerie atmosphere and the sense of distance between us. It seemed to me it would take a very long time to get to know her; an obliqueness would come between us; there would have to be a key and I should not find it. In this mystified state I could see two things clearly: her quality and her meticulousness.

I also thought I should not comprehend the particular symbolism within her. But when Len Lye's beautiful photomontages for the covers of her book came, it seemed to me that he was in perfect communion with what she was expressing, so well-fitting to the poems did they appear. Made of assembled fragments that might be found on some exotic or dream strand, these designs suggested nature's world in a sort of petrified permanence. On the front cover stood a tall figure in cork, with a long, feminine back, evoking an Egyptian form; all around lay an unidentifiable sea-trove that has seemingly passed through some mysterious ocean change, and there are other things of earth, water, and desert beautifully spread in a sort of timelessness. As with the poems and

their maker, the word for this could be "other world."
One of the best poems in the volume is called "Egypt."

> Yes, Egypt is still with us,
> Egypt, unopened tomb—
> And who does not lie there,
> A mummy yet undefiled—
> Who does not lie there,
> Who lives, who is human—
> Except the devil, the horned scarab,
> Sole petty monarch of the light
> While the great dead still sleep?
>
> But when the great dead at last live,
> What is Egypt then—
> When Nefertiti is more beautiful than a queen
> And the lachrymatory vessels are indeed full
> In the name not of empty sorrow?
>
> Egypt is then the devil's undisputed pit
> Which he, king of life before life was,
> Now populates with carcases,
> The souls of those who may not be
> Since the upper air is bespoken fairly
> And is not bottomless.

Laura Riding

Four Unposted Letters to Catherine

At that moment, Laura Riding's rhythm and reiterative use of words seemed much influenced by Gertrude Stein, although this was more noticeable in her next book published by the Hours Press, *Four Unposted Letters to Catherine*. However, Laura Riding's personality was very different from Miss Stein's and her influence could only be applicable (is it really so?) on account of a certain intentional repetition of words and the intentional simplification of statements—some of them straightforward, some of them subtle—which recall the Stein manner (once labelled "a Gargantuan stutter" by Wyndham Lewis). No stutter is there whatever in the thoughts and observations of Laura Riding as expressed here in her vision of how life should be, and of how it is often conducted. Her essays are in the form of letters to a child.

It would have been good if Laura Riding and Robert Graves had been in France in 1930, for I would have liked to know them better and to go over this book with them. They were, however, at their own Seizin Press in Mallorca, and the best I could do was to read the *Letters* many times, and while doing so, it seemed to me that her intent was increasingly clear; all was so simply stated, and I had been looking, at first (though why?), for inner meanings.

Rereading them just now confirms this, and it was also the reaction of Michael Roberts who, in *The Poetry Review*, wrote: "Give this volume to a child; it tells so simply, that an adult may find it difficult, how it is good to live straight, independently of the tortuous conventions of others: how there is a difference between the doing which tends towards the general comfort and that which people 'do, not for comfort or fun but in order to prove to themselves and to other people that they are people.' It shows, too, the difference between the knowing which starts with self-knowledge and the learning which is the acquisition of facts."

It was a time already of "hermetic" writing in much contemporary poetry, although French critics had not yet coined the expression "école hermétique," which one might translate as "sealed school," signifying that such poets were so much enclosed in their own meanings and images as to be inaccessible to most readers. Laura Riding, by now much esteemed as a poet of quality, ranked high among those considered difficult. In a long review by Herbert Palmer that has survived among my Hours Press papers, Palmer calls her "one of the most inexplicable of modern American poets," but then turns to *Four Unposted Letters to Catherine* and writes: "It is like going to a warm fire on a bitter cold day to turn to her very different *Four Unposted Letters to Catherine* which is for the most part charmingly and lucidly written, addressed to a child, full of downright truths and wisdom, and such flashes of insight as 'Making a poem is like being alive for always.' Though even in this book the anarchist or overbearing feminist sometimes gets too much on the top, as in 'The greatest showers-off and busybodies are men. And so the world is ruled by men, because it is a world not of doing but of over-doing.' The final part of that is finely and truly said, but the rest is wrong, especially as women are quite as much the cause of over-doing in the world as are the men."

Certainly nothing could be more clear and direct than the following lines from the *Letters*:

> There is no limit to what people can learn if they want to. It is the easiest thing possible. It is easier than doing and it is easier than thinking. It is not real. Well, then, what is the good of learning? The good of learning is this: that it can clear up doing that is real doing. . . . Learning can be a bridge between doing and thinking. But then there is a danger that the person who uses learning may get stuck in learning and never get on to thinking. . . . People get wisdom from thinking not from learning, and thinking is being just yourself. And when you are yourself as much as you can be, then you know all about as much as yourself is. . . . Nature is what is there, regardless of what you say or don't say. If you like you can forget all about it. You can treat it as if it wasn't there. Indeed, if you are occupied in being yourself, you can rely on its being there to relax into. And you can always shake yourself out of it again, and it won't have made any difference one way or the other, for or against you, for or against nature.

And it was Richard Aldington, writing in *The Referee*, who confirmed my impressions: "Miss Riding gives me the feeling of someone thinking aloud and very intensely. The simplicity and directness are very pleasing."

The covers made for this volume in small format are another pair of beautiful photomontages by Len Lye, which, if they suggest stonelike figures and a sort of arabesque, also evoke the thought of tapestry and Renaissance velvet, strange as it seems to accord such very different things.

Samuel Beckett

Whoroscope

Before his long stay in the United States, Richard Aldington had become a good friend of the Hours Press, and I think he was pleased with my production of *The Eaten Heart.* He was ever full of ideas for me to take up, and certainly the most rewarding was the suggestion of a poetry competition. "Why not offer a prize for the best poem on a certain subject? In that way new talent might be discovered and it would get the press even better known." "On what subject?" I asked, immediately interested. "Let us make it a poem on Time—on any aspect of Time." There must obviously be a limit as to length, we agreed, else someone will find it possible (using pen or pencil rather than typewriter) to send in something half the length of the *Iliad.* Up to one-hundred lines seemed a good, generous length.

The announcement, quickly printed in red ink on a small square card, went out to the literary reviews in England and elsewhere. It read: "Nancy Cunard, Hours Press, in collaboration with Richard Aldington, offers £10 for the best poem up to 100 lines, in english or american on TIME (for or against). Entries up to June 15, 1930." It was not a very large prize, yet, one reflected, it might be won by four perfect lines or some exquisite rhyming epigram, just as well as by a sonnet-sequence or a blank or free verse narrative.

Well can I remember now how that large hall at Le Puits Carré looked in 1930, with its open windows and doors, where so much long, cold winter work of circularizing and addressing was done. My advertisements, I recall, usually formed a circle on the floor around the stove. Today, however, it was nearly mid-summer and Aldington and I were at Le Puits Carré to read and judge the entries we had received in such abundance, nearly one-hundred of them. One always arrived at Réanville from Rue Guenégaud laden with proofs and papers and a large amount of correspondence. No weekends were ever free of work, but it was doubly possible to achieve in the quiet of the pleasant house. In the course of the last month all the entries had arrived at the press, many of them in handwriting, which does not make for clarity. As we read them aloud to each other (we would later reread them, or most of them, to ourselves for more criticism and then confer together again), we were frankly disappointed. Nothing here, save perhaps two or three? And not even those were good, said Aldington. Yes, on the whole, they were very mediocre when not frankly bad. The collection ranged from doggerel to a kind of sham metaphysics, and not one was by anyone who was known as a poet, or in the opinion of my fellow judge, who could remotely be called one. I remember nothing of any of them now, except our disappointment. Sadly the prize would have to go to one of those two or three. Or could there yet be a miracle? Three or four days were left.

And a miracle there was. It came to the Rue Guenégaud after closing time on the last night of the contest and was found by me the next morning where it had been slipped under the door: across the cover of a small folder was written *Whoroscope*; beneath was the name Samuel Beckett. His name meant nothing to either Aldington or myself. The poem, on the other hand, meant a very great deal, even on the first, feverish read-through. What remarkable lines, what images and analogies, what vivid coloring throughout; indeed, what technique! This long poem, mysterious, obscure in parts, centered around Descartes, was clearly by someone very intellectual and highly educated.

Our enthusiasm was great, and the fact of its having arrived at the last moment made it all the sweeter. The obscurities in the poem were of the kind that meant that one could not be in full command of the subject—the events in the life of Descartes and his times. But perhaps the difficulty could be overcome, without detracting from the poem, by appending a series of notes.

Immediately summoned, Samuel Beckett quickly arrived and what he told me about the way this intense poem had been composed struck me as astounding. For the fact is that *Whoroscope*, which has ninety-eight lines, is very intricate in thought and composition. Yet, he said, he had known nothing of the competition till the very last afternoon. The first half of the poem he had written before dinner; then came "a guzzle of salad and Chambertin at the Cochon de Lait." Afterwards he had gone back to the Ecole Normale Supérieure to finish it. "About three in the morning it was done, and I walked down to the Rue Guenégaud and put it in your box." What other words exist for this but inspiration and virtuosity?

To those curious to know what Samuel Beckett looked like at this time, in the summer of 1930, I will say that he has changed very little, if at all, in outline, and that his personality seems to me now yet more vivid. He is very tall and slim to leanness, of handsome aquiline features, and there is something now in his face of the fierce austerity of a Mexican eagle. But why Mexican? It seems to be a combination of two things: the natural eagle and something akin to the pre-Columbian sculpture of the Mexican Indians. He is a man of stone, you think until he speaks, and then all is warmth if he be with someone sympathetic to him. He is fair, with a direct gaze at times coming to pinpoint precision in his light blue eyes. There was then, and there is now, a feeling of the spareness of the desert about him, which, somehow, has its own kind of harmony. He is very self-assured in a deep, quiet way, unassuming in manner, and interested in mankind, despite all the despair in his plays, which, to me, are imbued with the strange paradox of compassion-contempt. One would not call him aloof but very self-contained. If you think he is looking slightly severe, this may be because he is assessing what has just been said, and his laughter and ease of manner are frank and swift. He is enchantingly Irish and, at that time on first seeing him, I thought there was just a touch here of the silhouette of James Joyce.

After our slightly halting first words—for I was so impressed by his poem I could not voice my admiration of it properly—we talked of more general things. Yes, though only twenty-four he had been living in Paris since 1928, but did not know very many of the French writers as yet. Someone had just brought the competition to his notice, and he thought he had not the slightest chance of winning it. I assured him the poem would be in print very shortly, and how glad Aldington and I were at having made contact with him. Who, I wondered, did we know in common? Why, Joyce, to be sure. Beckett was in fact

Nancy Cunard and Henry Crowder in the Hours Press,
Paris 1930

doing some research work for the author of *Ulysses*. At that time, Joyce was occupied with *Work in Progress* and, because of his poor eyesight, had asked Beckett and other friends to look up all kinds of strange data. He never became Joyce's secretary, which is the story that has generally gone around, but, along with others, he was assisting Joyce by reading and marking passages he might use. Did he not tell me later that he was once requested by Joyce to furnish the names of all the rivers in Europe? Can it have been all, or of those in one of the European countries?

I suppose James Joyce was my most famous visitor at Rue Guenégaud, and maybe if the press had gone on longer it would have been my honor to publish a short work by him. This looked as if it might be so. It was his idea, and sounded somewhat in the nature of a bargain which he though we might conclude together.

However little one knew him one felt, I think, his tenacity of purpose, and this was all the more evident on account of the reason which brought him to me that summer day in 1930. It was his desire and intention to befriend the Irish singer John Sullivan. And it was the second time he had come to see me for the same purpose.

I had never been introduced to Joyce, although we had many friends in common, such as Wyndham Lewis, Ezra Pound, T. S. Eliot, Robert McAlmon, and others, yet there he was suddenly, unannounced, a few days earlier in my room at the Hotel Crystal, myself in bed with an abcess in the throat, practically speechless with pain. The knock on the door revealed a tall, austere figure whose hands went faltering after some piece of furniture, for he was nearly blind already.

"I am James Joyce," he announced, "and I have come to

talk to you about something it seems to me it is your duty to accomplish." He appeared so nearly blind that I wondered in consternation how he came to be out alone like this, and helped him to a chair. It made one shudder to think of him alone with his stick in the crowded streets of Paris.

The "duty" was immediately forthcoming. Now, said he, my mother, Lady Cunard, then in Paris, was a very great friend of Sir Thomas Beecham, the conductor, who was also in Paris at that time. Now, in Paris likewise was the great Irish singer, Sullivan, who should be heard at once by Sir Thomas and engaged to sing in grand opera in Britain. Now, I must use my influence with my mother to arrange for a hearing. To assure Joyce that he himself would have much more influence with her, and Beecham too, than anything that could come from me seemed to annoy him. She would listen to me, he said, and I told him as firmly that she would not. Joyce knew her personally and she had already befriended him. I told him I would certainly transmit his hope, but that things would be far more effectively handled if he would get in touch with her himself. And again I was sorry to see that Joyce did not believe me when I spoke the truth, having no influence with her whatsoever. And so that morning had passed.

And then, as unexpectedly, he came to the press a few days later. It was towards evening and several of us were there, although I cannot remember just who. I know we ran forward to greet him. Would he not take a drink with us in our local bistro, perhaps even have dinner? I assured him that his request had been transmitted but could not say if it had been taken into account. My mother had seemed to understand and had said she would tell Beecham, but there was nothing definite to go on, and, really, he himself should get in touch with her. It was he, great and esteemed, who would be so much more likely to be listened to. Meanwhile, would he not sit and have a little drink with us? No, he would not. He was gracious if, as I found him, very conventional and rather difficult to talk to. The point was Sullivan, who *must* be engaged for grand opera. Could I not realize the urgency of this? If I had tried already, I should try now much harder. He went on saying what a fine singer was Sullivan, and that it was shocking he should not have gained due recognition, and then he used the word "duty" again. As he left, he dropped more than a hint that if Sullivan were engaged, well, some piece of work suitable to the Hours might come my way. In the end, it seems to me that Sullivan was not engaged, though Beecham did hear him, and in any case the press closed down the next year.

Not for nothing did Samuel Beckett impress me as one of those strikingly intellectual faces one would turn round to look at in a street. He was already a very fine linguist as well as a scholar (Trinity College, Dublin). His Italian was beautiful, sound, and exact, and he spoke it with the right accent and had read much Italian literature. His German was excellent, and his French well on the way to what it later became. He is now one of those extremely rare authors who is completely bi-lingual, down to the last detail, in English and French, as he has shown in several books and plays written in the latter, which he has put into English and which have been acted in London and elsewhere after long runs in Paris. His modesty was and is palpable and is part of his self-containedness—the humility of the true artist. I thought of him at once, I remember, as a very sincere artist indeed.

As to *Whoroscope*, he readily agreed that there should be

notes. He quickly wrote them and they were printed at the end of the poem, which I thought greatly increased its clarity and consecutiveness. The personality of this poem has remained absolutely intact and to me it is one of the most striking of its epoch. How gratefully we gave him the £10 reward. *Whoroscope* was quickly set by hand and printed in Caslon 11-point with notes in smaller type. A small banner across the cover announced that *Whoroscope* was the Hours Press prize winning poem. I am told that the 5s signed edition is now worth £5 a copy. It had good reviews and sold well and there were no hitches before the handsome new item, in dull scarlet covers with black lettering, was placed in the front window of the Rue Guénégaud.

Such was the beginning of a long friendship with Samuel Beckett, who later translated a considerable number of articles from the French for my *Negro Anthology*, but whom I lost sight of completely during the course of the last war. He stayed in France. Having an Irish passport he could have claimed complete detachment, but this was by no means the case. Indeed, the opposite was true; he took sides to some purpose and this counted effectively in the Allied war effort.

The spectacular and merited rise to fame of Samuel Beckett dates from ten or eleven years ago and began, of course, in France. The honor of being the first to print him (with what pleasure I say this), comes to me, for *Whoroscope* was his first separately published work. How delighted I am to reproduce the poem here.

What's that?
An egg?
By the brothers Boot it stinks fresh.

Give it to Gillot.

Galileo how are you
and his consecutive thirds!
The vile old Copernican lead-swinging son of a
    sutler!
We're moving he said we're off-Porca
    Madonna!
the way a boatswain would be, or a sack-of-
    potatoey charging Pretender.
That's not moving, that's *moving*.

What's that?
A little green fry or a mushroomy one?
Two lashed ovaries with prostisciutto?
How long did she womb it, the feathery one?
Three days and four nights?
Give it to Gillot.

Faulhaber, Beeckman and Peter the Red,
come now in the cloudy avalanche or Gassendi's
    sun-red crystally cloud
and I'll pebble you all your hen-and-a-half ones
or I'll pebble a lens under the quilt in the midst
    of day.

To think he was my own brother, Peter the
    Bruiser,
and not a syllogism out of him
no more than if Pa were still in it.
Hey! pass over those coppers,
    sweet millèd sweat of my burning liver!
Them were the days I sat in the hot-cupboard
    throwing Jesuits out of the skylight.

These Were the Hours

Who's that? Hals?
Let him wait.

My squinty doaty!
I hid and you sook.
And Francine my precious fruit of a house-and-
 parlour foetus!
What an exfoliation!
Her little grey flayed epidermis and scarlet
 tonsils!
My one child
scourged by a fever to stagnant murky blood-
blood!
Oh Harvey belovèd
how shall the red and white, the many in the
 few,
(dear bloodswirling Harvey)
eddy through that cracked beater?
And the fourth Henry came to the crypt of the
 arrow.

What's that?
How long?
Sit on it.

A wind of evil flung my despair of ease
against the sharp spires of the one
 lady:
not once or twice but . . .
(Kip of Christ hatch it!)
in one sun's drowning
(Jesuitasters please copy).
So on with the silk hose over the knitted, and

the morbid leather-
what am I saying! the gentle canvas-
and away to Ancona on the bright Adriatic,
and farewell for a space to the yellow key of
   the Rosicrucians.
They don't know what the master of them that
   do did,
that the nose is touched by the kiss of all foul
   and sweet air,
and the drums, and the throne of the faecal
   inlet,
and the eyes by its zig-zags.
So we drink Him and eat Him
and the watery Beaune and the stale cubes of
   Hovis
because He can jig
as near or as far from His Jigging Self
and as sad or lively as the chalice or the tray asks.
How's that, Antonio?
In the name of Bacon will you chicken me up
   that egg.
Shall I swallow cave-phantoms?

Anna Maria!
She reads Moses and says her love is crucified.
Leider! Leider! she bloomed and withered,
a pale abusive parakeet in a mainstreet window.

No I believe every word of it I assure you.
Fallor, ergo sum!
The coy old frôleur!
He tolle'd and legge'd
and he buttoned on his redemptorist waistcoat.

These Were the Hours

No matter, let it pass.
I'm a bold boy I know
so I'm not my son
(even if I were a concierge)
nor Joachim my father's
but the chip of a perfect block that's neither old
    nor new,
the lonely petal of a great high bright rose.
Are you ripe at last,
my slim pale double-breasted turd?
How rich she smells,
this abortion of a fledgling!
I will eat it with a fish fork.

White and yolk and feathers.
Then I will rise and move moving
toward Rahab of the snows,
the murdering matinal pope-confessed amazon,
Christina the ripper.
Oh Weulles spare the blood of a Frank
who has climbed the bitter steps,
(René du Perron . . .!)
and grant me my second
starless inscrutable hour.

Ezra Pound

I saw Ezra Pound first, and with what surprise, for his appearance was astonishing, as were his manner and mannerisms, at a tea table in London, in 1915, that of my mother, to whom he came almost daily at one time to talk to her about James Joyce and Wyndham Lewis. Urgent was the need, said he, for financial aid to be given Joyce while at work on the lengthy writing of *Ulysses*, and this led to Joyce's receiving, soon after, a grant from "The King's Bounty." Pound was concerned about Wyndham Lewis too, who was at that time at a particularly dangerous sector of the front and was far too good an artist, said Pound, to risk being sacrificed, as had been the magnificent sculptor, Gaudier Brzeska, who had been killed fighting while still very young. Lewis should be entrusted with chronicling the war pictorially, and soon after he was nominated one of the war artists.

That appearance of his in 1915! He was of middle stature, with green, lynx-like eyes, a head of thick, waving red hair and a pointed red beard. He was dressed at that time in black and white check trousers, black velvet jacket, with a large-brimmed black felt hat. He wore a sweeping black cape and carried yellow chamois leather gloves and a cane. Thus he looked singularly like Rodolfo in "La Boheme." Be it said that the second large painting Wyndham Lewis made of him in the winter of 1938–39, which is in the Tate Gallery, is a fine likeness. But even more interesting is what must be called the "premature death-mask" which, for a hoax, Pound had made of himself and distributed sometime during the mid-twenties.

His personality, especially when met for the first time, could be alarming to some, and his often elliptic way of speaking, of putting already subtle thoughts or images into such original perspectives made him seem "difficult." Vibrating and dynamic he was, and he could certainly become ecstatic. What can better illustrate this than the extraordinary moment that occurred one night when I was with him and his wife in Rome? We had been dining, and how well, in the Ulpia, where the strength of those admirable Vini Castelli Romani wines suddenly impelled him to break into Greek, to the delight of the manager and waiters gathered round, who hung on to every incomprehensible word in encouraging if amazed assembly. On and on went the spate of the mysterious peroration, accompanied by flowering gestures of emphasis; the rhythm of it all fascinated; it was, indeed, unique.

By the time the *Cantos* began to appear, Ezra Pound had already written much poetry and prose, made many translations and done several books of criticism. He could be considered one of the living classics. The subjects he had written of ranged from Confucius to the work of Guido Cavalcanti. Music was another interest. He wrote an opera on Villon and his book on George Antheil, the American composer, *Antheil and the Treatise on Harmony*, published by the Three Mountains Press, is well known. he was among the very first to proclaim the excellence

THE HOURS PRESS

New Works by

EZRA POUND
R. ALDINGTON
ROBERT GRAVES
LAURA RIDING
WALTER LOWENFELS
ROY CAMPBELL
HAROLD ACTON
BOB BROWN
BRIAN HOWARD

Music by

HENRY CROWDER

is now at

15, RUE GUÉNÉGAUD

PARIS 6e

Tel. Littré 50-03

Nancy Cunard

Post card announcement of the new address of the Hours Press

of Joyce and Eliot. A French critic called him "the greatest creator of innovations and poetical experiences." The bibliography of Ezra Pound is indeed vast and diverse.

Pound's book on his close friend, Gaudier Brzeska, is full of admirable criticism, and he was ever active and generous in his desire to help win recognition for writers and artists whom he considered worthwhile. One realized that he was a thorough revolutionary, intellectually and artistically, and an intensely creative man, pre-eminently a maker, entirely personal. There was a good deal of "panache" to him, a certain flamboyance, and not everyone was able to appreciate his "learned blasts" (as one critic put it). His knowledge of literature, ancient and modern, can hardly be questioned, if his true scholarship was sometimes denied. He drew his subjects from many different cultures—from the classics, Chinese, Japanese, ancient Provencal, the Troubadours, and Italy. His knowledge of certain regions in France was astonishing, for he had often travelled on foot through them; he found enjoyment in how many places, gathering knowledge from how many things. He was then, in fact, a man of great appetite intellectually, of driving energy—and doubtless is so now.

There is a theory about why Ezra Pound turned Fascist, even to the point of broadcasting on Radio Roma during World War II. And it is a theory told to me by Ernest Hemingway, whom I met in Havana in 1941 when I was trying to get back to England. I remember nearly tripping over his great foot stuck out on the sidewalk, looking up annoyed and being greeted by Hemingway's broad smile We celebrated with drinks and I asked him about Ezra. Why did he think Pound had gone Fascist? Hemingway never spoke more charmingly and gently. He said that

127

Ezra had been ridiculed or paid no attention to first of all in his native country, the United States. Next, living in England, he had not encountered sufficient respect for his work and ideas. Thirdly, it was more or less the same when he went to live in France. But in Italy, where he settled in the mid-twenties, he was considered of importance increasingly as the years passed. There he was a figure, perhaps even "a great man." To those of us who knew and highly appreciated him in the past, this fascism is inexplicable. Detestable as it is, this political aspect of Pound should never make one "cheat" against him, by which I mean the fact remains—and it cannot be obliterated—that his creativeness, technique, and the sum total of his poetical work make him a great poet. How the two things can be reconciled I do not know. They simply cannot be, and yet both are there in one living man.

One would have thought that, to someone so hyper-sensitive, the very vulgarity of fascism would have been repugnant, even leaving out entirely its fundamental principles. I have known Ezra Pound to be a very human kind of person, for example when he replied to an appeal I circulated in the early thirties asking for funds to aid the defense council of the Scottsboro boys. The appeal took the form of a brief history of the case, emphasizing that the trial had been farcical and that an appeal for a second trial had finally been won after great effort. At the end of my circular, I wrote: "If you are against the lynching and terrorisation of the most oppressed race in the world, if you have any innate sense of justice, sign this protest and contribute towards the defense funds." Though gathering signatures of writers and intellectuals was only a small part of the work I did for the Scottsboro case, it was gratifying to receive so many replies. Gide, Aragon, Breton,

Beckett, Bryher, Richard Church, Antheil, Sinclair
Lewis, Janet Flanner, and many, many others sent back
signed forms almost immediately. And among them
came one from Ezra and Dorothy Pound. At the bottom
Ezra had appended this note: "I not only protest, but if
this sort of judicial sanction of murder and frame-up
continues, I should be disposed to advocate direct action.
We have had enough criminals in high office already.
A state even a state sanely founded can not indefinitely
continue if it condones and sanctions legal murder of
innocent men."

Then later, some years after we had had our dealings
over the volume of *Cantos*, he became very anti-Semitic,
and I received a letter from him in the middle of the
Ethiopian War telling me he hoped I realized that "the
Abyssinians are BLACK JEWS." With all his humanity,
so well remembered from the times I knew him first, this
fascism is totally baffling. His is, indeed, "a case," an
utterly insoluble one.

The full title of Pound's Hours Press book is, somewhat
modestly, *A Draft of XXX Cantos*, but the assertion found
by Ezra Pound himself for its announcement card was
"Eliminating the idea that his knowledge of the past has
invalidated his perception of the present."

Collectors of his work and of private press books will
remember with admiration the two beautiful editions of
these same cantos in large format (very restricted in number of copies) which were produced in the mid-twenties,
the first half of them by William Bird at the Three Mountains Press in Paris; the second half, slightly later, by John
Rodker at the Ovid Press in London. My own edition,
in ordinary format, combined the two and is the first
printing of all the thirty cantos ready at that date.

The scope of them is enormous; in general idea they have been compared to Dante's *Inferno*. The subjects and the allusions to people and situations belong to many lands and different historical periods and civilizations. All of this makes it often difficult to seize or properly follow the poet's intention. Yet there is great beauty in many of the lines, and several of the *Cantos* contain long sequences that deal, more or less, with the same figures, the same time-epoch. His earlier poetry was more restricted in subject. The *Cantos* roam from land to land and century to century. I once asked Ezra if he thought any *one* person would be capable of recognizing *all* the references and allusions. He laughed and shook his head, and said: "Waal, perhaps some learned old *Turkish* scholar, someone like that." At times the *Cantos* are so filled with personal notings as to appear secret. Then suddenly, like a limpid, contained stream, will come a long, consecutive passage. For instance, Canto XLV (which is in the New Directions volume of the 85 *Cantos*), the one on Usura, is all of a piece, a very violin in the hands of a virtuoso, rising out of the explosive Pound world.

It is interesting to reread the two appreciations of Ezra Pound's poetical work, by Basil Bunting and Dudley Fitts respectively. In the searching analysis that Bunting gives him, the following lines throw light on the *Cantos*: "The parallel with Dante is obvious, and obviously in the poet's mind. The *Divine Comedy* is a world built of thousands of individual instances classified and correlated. The *Cantos* take their matter here and there, at first it seems haphazardly; but order is beginning to show in the great conglomeration. The fact of correlation is already clear, if not yet the principle it is based on. To illustrate, comment, contrast, organize, the Good Life is presumably the object of the poem, as of Dante's."

Dudley Fitts wrote an equally perceptive analysis, from which this extract is also illuminating: "Less invalid than the 'unintelligibility' criticism, though by no means sound, is the objection that an extraordinary apparatus of historical and literary erudition is necessary for the enjoyment of the *Cantos*. It is obvious that a tremendous amount of factual knowledge has gone into the making of the poem. Historical documentation, ranging over time and space, involving literatures and mythologies familiar and unfamiliar, recording events of universal significance with an emphasis neither lesser nor greater than that accorded to the narration of imaginary or purely personal events—this is one of the devices of the poems: a major device, to be sure, but not more than a device." Later on comes this: "His method is identification of period with period, of personality with personality, in a continual present. He is not an archeologist or an historian, though archeology and history serve his devices. His periods and his personages are exactly what he has called them—*personae*, masks, of his own time and his own personality."

The production of *XXX Cantos* went smoothly. The length of the book made it too complicated to print at the Rue Guenégaud. It was Pound himself who found Maître-Imprimeur Bernouard, in Paris, and told him exactly how he wanted the volume to look. To my mind it is perfect in taste and it was beautifully turned out from the technical point of view. It bears his name as well as the imprint of the Hours, and each canto is embellished by one of the handsome initials drawn expressly by Dorothy Shakespear, the American poet's wife. In fact, it was the great American book-collector, Herbert L. Rothchild, one of my best clients in the United States, who paid tribute to the production and to the Hours Press by reproducing the first page of the fourth canto in his *Contemporary Presses, A Survey* (1931), which contained examples of the work then being done by private presses in America, England, and Europe.

Roy Campbell

Poems

Meeting Roy Campbell in London for the first time in
1919, or so, in the Brasserie of the Café Royal (then in its
prime) was the fulfillment of a promise repeatedly made
me by the poet and critic T. W. Earp, who had so often
exclaimed about the wonderful new poet he called "The
Zulu." Tommy Earp, one of the most learned and individual of Oxford men, was a great admirer of this young
poet; he seemed to have been bowled over by him
personally, and predicted great things for Campbell if he
would cultivate his talent for verse. So the three of us sat
drinking together a moment that morning, but my impression of "The Zulu" was imprecise, amounting to
"this is something of a dark horse." I could see the charm
within his quiet manner, the vigor concentrated then in
his dark eyes, which now and again would flash. He was
vivacious, yet seemed a little shy, or reserved, and con-
trasted much in appearance with the fair-haired, precise,
high-voiced Earp. He was South African born, had
recently arrived from his homeland, and had already made
many friends in England. Definitely a personality while
yet so young, Campbell, I suppose, can now be rated one
of the most "picturesque" figures among the poets of our
time; that will be one verdict. Earp radiated admiration

for Roy's poetry: "We should see, oh, indeed yes, we should see that this was going to turn into someone to be reckoned with." His predictions were frequently voiced; Roy had obviously been a "rich find."

I knew him little, on the whole, but many were the accounts from this one and that one throughout the years of how his personality developed. To some he became "rumbuctious" (he was indeed slashing in his satires—but what else is satire for?); sometimes he was out for trouble; the "he-man" strain in him developed mightily and grew upon him, I thought. Although I do not remember seeing him actually aggressive, he had the reputation of being at times quarrelsome and overbearing and full of threats. The row with Stephen Spender has been called "the permanent row." Another went on with Hugh MacDiarmid. John Gawsworth took his defense, and no doubt his real friends found him warmhearted as well as sometimes hasty. He was frequently swashbuckling. It was not thus I ever saw him, although I have certainly read him in that mood. However, the fact remains that he has left much interesting poetry, prose, and translations.

At the time of the Hours Press volume in 1930, he must have been about thirty years old and had already written considerably and well. His rise to fame years before with *The Flaming Terrapin* had been spectacular, and later *The Wayzgoose* also evoked great appreciation. His autobiography was vivid. In him, I thought, were currents of generosity and bitterness. His poetry is far indeed from the several schools and influences of his time and it runs and leaps with its own particular surge.

Soon "the dark horse" (others too had thought of him this way) had become Roy Campbell, swinger of powerful lines. Good at rhyming, full of fire, high in color, rich in

HOURS PRESS
HOURS PRESS
HOURS PRESS

15 Rue Guénégaud
PARIS 6e
Tel. Littré 50-03

New works by living authors. Signed, numbered and limited
editions privately printed.

POETRY	E	PROSE

E
Z
R
A

P
O
U
N
D

*

C
O
L
L
E
C
T
E
D

POETRY

Walter Lowenfels
Apollinaire. An Elegy
150 signed copies £ 1.10.

Robert Graves
Ten Poems More
200 signed copies £ 1.10.

Laura Riding
Twenty Poems Less
200 signed copies £ 1.10.

Bob Brown
Words. Cover by Man Ray
150 signed copies £ 1.10.

Harold Acton
This Chaos.
150 signed copies £ 1.10.

Roy Campbell
Poems

Brian Howard
First Poems

PROSE

Richard Aldington
A War Story
300 signed copies £ 2.

Laura Riding
Four Unposted Letters
to Catherine.
200 signed copies £ 2.

MUSIC

Henry Crowder
Six Piano Pieces with
poems by Richard Al-
dington Walter Lowen-
fels and Nancy Cunard.

Covers by Frank
Dobson, Eugene Mac
Cown, Man Ray, Yves
Tanguy, Hilaire Hiler,
Elliott Seabrooke.

CANTOS
in One Volume
200 Copies £ 2.

The Hours Press list of new works

ornament and imagery, dexterous, eloquent, the dash in him not excluding craft and what is well wrought—such are characteristics of his poetry. He was also a good translator of French and Spanish poems. (Was the latter perhaps when, leaving France, he went to live in Spain?)

Perhaps because I never knew him well, he was to me a bewildering person and contradictory. It might have been that, as a South African white man, he would have been afflicted with race prejudice, but nothing of the kind was apparent. Indeed, the very opposite was true when Henry Crowder and I visited him in 1930 for an enchanting afternoon in his little house near Marseille. He was then living at Martigues, for quite a time also the home of Augustus John, who was a close friend of Campbell's. I have nothing but good memories of that day, and of our literary dealings which were as easy as could be. He certainly talked to me with enthusiasm about the African Negroes.

But my surprise was very great indeed when, as a journalist in Madrid at the start of the Spanish Civil War, in October 1936, I heard from friends that Campbell was actually with the Nationalist and Moorish troops then approaching Toledo. He had been living in Spain for several years and had learned the language well, making translations of highly complex contemporary Spanish poetry. Somehow, I cannot visualize him actually liking the company of Fascist generals and bankers rather than that—so much more alive and authentic—of "the common people" and the many artists and writers who were so preponderantly Republican. Yet espouse Franco's cause he did. His long poem, written then, *Flowering Rifle, A Poem from the Battlefield of Spain,* purports to be about the war but is mainly a collection of diatribes against "Jews and Marxists," and seems to me a tub-thumping, lengthy piece of boredom. No matter how unsympathetic, the poem might perhaps have been revealing and interesting had it contained merely a few facts. The Spanish Republican intellectuals were stupefied at learning that he was outside Toledo with the rebel troops. They had to be content later with realizing that he *was* an exception among the predominantly anti-Franco intellectuals of Great Britain, and, for that matter, of most of the world. I continue to find it strange that Campbell (whom I had thought of as "a generous nature"—to put it in three words) should have chosen the side, and all its contents, the least in keeping with what seemed to be his own loyalty to freedom, individuality, and creativeness. That he wanted to be with Franco has been commented on by some of his old friends in England as derived from "his need of excitement," which to my mind is an irresponsible analysis. Another explanation, lightly tossed at me by the painter Nina Hamnett, who knew him, I think, very well, was Catholicism. "That is where it has led him," she said, which left me rather surprised.

But all this was years ahead of our dealings with his volume at the Hours. At that time I had not seen him since the early London days, but in reading his hefty and often beautiful lines, I could well imagine the vigorous personality he had, by all accounts, become. Near Martigues he was often engaged in water-jousting, an ancient sport of the Mediterranean. One would think that, like gondoliering, it would be a hard thing for someone to acquire who has not learned it practically from a child up. But Campbell was proficient at it. He was also one for the bullring, although Spaniards hold it is impossible for such a tall man ever to become a *torero*, especially if he has

138

not trained at an early age and is, moreover, a foreigner. Be that as it may, Campbell was certainly often in some kind of bullfight, for there are several varieties.

At this time, apart from being a man of such strong physical appetites, he was also writing a great deal. No less than six books of various lengths were to come out shortly, one of them being *The Georgiad*, two sections of which he gave me for the Hours Press volume.

His name was such that his *Poems* (there were but twelve) was oversubscribed far before publication and—as in the case of Robert Graves—my delight was great at being able to send him royalties of £80 or so. The *Poems* made a handsome volume in my usual poetry format, bound in Vermilion paper boards, with two drawings by Campbell himself on the covers. On the front is a mounted cavalier with a lance charging a bull; on the back, an olive tree caught by the wind; both of them simple yet effective.

The two poems on "The Olive Tree" greatly pleased the critic of *The Observer*, who wrote: "In the few poems elaborately produced by the Hours Press, Mr. Roy Campbell makes a definite advance on 'Adamastor.' But here, particularly in the two poems on 'The Olive Tree,' he approaches to the quiet without which all poetry is the crackling of thorns."

THE OLIVE TREE

In a bare country shorn of leaf,
    By no remote sierra screened,
Where pauses in the wind are brief
    As the remorses of a fiend,
The stark Laocoon this tree
    Forms of its knotted arm and thigh

> In snaky tussle with a sky
>   Whose hatred is eternity,
> Through his white fronds that whirl and seethe
>   And in the groaning root he screws,
> Makes heard the cry of all who breathe
>   Repulsing and accusing still
> The Enemy who shaped his thews
>   And in inherent to his will.

A small photograph of Campbell has survived, a mere snapshot which shows him standing on the high back part of a boat, with his long lance poised and ready for the water-jousting. On the back of this he wrote and thanked me for the edition of his *Poems*. "The book is wonderfully done. I am only afraid that the poems are too insignificant to justify printing. Come and see us if you have a car. There are two quiet pubs in Martigues. We have just won the championship of the Mediterranean, with plenty of prize money. There was nearly a riot in Marseille. Thanks very much for the books. I shall send you some better work afterward."

John Rodker

Collected Poems

From the time of his association, while still very young, with the imagist group, John Rodker was recognized as a poet of great intensity and sincerity. Possessed of much education and well read, he was one of the original imagists and highly intellectual. Of a thoughtful, analytical disposition, I remember those sudden, wild contradictions within him, as if an argument had been going on all too long in there, until the owner of both threw up his hands, so to speak, with "a plague on both your houses." Was it partly the fact that he was half Polish that made him so introspective, sometimes brooding and self-critical to the point of self-torture? The characteristics of his nature come out strongly in his poems. He would occasionally say to me (for we knew each other well for some time) how he felt uncertain of himself, and how much doubt—too much—there was in the modern world. Intensely conscientious, he was, I think, one of the most self-critical people I have ever met. But then, his sense of humor, suddenly again ascendant, would bring back the sunlight; and his appreciation of beauty, calculated or accidental, here, there, and everywhere, was spontaneous and authentic. He could be, and generally was, a most enchanting companion and several were the journeys we took together, namely to Italy, where we visited Ezra Pound at Rapallo and Norman Douglas in Florence, and many a picture gallery and many a Roman ruin. There was also a fine walking tour in southwest France.

Long before I knew him he had been a conscientious objector during the First World War. Being sent to Dartmoor for several arduous, even terrible months, led to a bitter description of the place in his book called *Dartmoor* and in "Two Prison Poems" printed in *Collected Poems*. Years later, a novel called *Adolphe 1920* revealed more of his complex nature. His poems bear witness to the battleground within, and all its "yea and nay" that led him, in the middle twenties, to be deeply concerned with psychoanalysis.

In the early twenties he founded his publishing house, the Casanova Society, which produced very fine work, such as the many volumes of *Casanova's Memoirs*, translated by Arthur Machen, and a set of *The Arabian Nights*, put into beautiful English by William Powys Mathers. It became famous among the bibliophiles and its works were much collected. One may say that his edition of some of Ezra Pound's *Cantos*, in very large, noble format, bound in green vellum, is one of the finest looking volumes ever published. He had learned printing and publishing years before at his Ovid Press, in London, which he had founded "to bring before the public work that was considered advanced." Its first book was T. S. Eliot's *Ara Vus Prec*, of which 264 copies were brought out in a fine and very individual format, on beautiful paper with initials and colophon by E. A. Wadsworth. Eliot's poems appeared in December, 1919; the following April Ezra Pound's *Hugh Selwyn Mauberly* was published.

142

John Rodker

If one half of him was bound to printing and publishing, the other half was certainly dedicated to poetry and fine writing. Though stern, he was an excellent critic and also a fine translator. One of the best things he has left is the admirable translation of *Les Chants de Maldoror*, by de Lautréamont, published by him at the Casanova Society.

At times insufficient money hampered bringing out his sumptuous editions, a difficulty that went unnoticed of his clients who were "by subscription only." To me he was helpful indeed when I began to learn printing, and had we been living in the same country maybe we should have done some work together. As it is, the Hours Press edition of his *Collected Poems* is the only volume of the Hours not to have been printed in France; its production (a pleasing one) Rodker supervised at the Curwen Press in England and then sent the books to me. The covers are striking compositions, photographic designs by Len Lye, which look as if they had been modelled in wax, with a graceful, semi-Egyptian influence. The initial lettering to the poems, designed by Edward Wadsworth, is the same as that used for *The Seven Pillars of Wisdom*, by Lawrence of Arabia. Of this volume *The Observer* wrote: "The Hours Press has lent Mr. John Rodker a fastidiously elegant habit."

From the work of fourteen years, Rodker selected twenty-one poems for this volume, which he introduced in a very personal and interesting preface.

For this book I have chosen such of my poems as best seem to me to have come off. Those omitted were too forced, or did not satisfy my present standards. One thing this collection makes me realise very clearly is how much influenced I was by the French poetry of 1850–1910. That was because I first came to poetry through that language (the foreign-ness already evocative and moving, which with its

These Were the Hours

content satisfied my particular demand for what poetry ought to be). But until this had happened I was closed to English poetry, so that perhaps later it was too late to write poetry that would be nearer the tradition of the language I was using. "Pieta," however, seems to me to have some of the good things of both languages. One gratifying thing about these poems is that they do get better with the years, but I have to ask myself why after 1925 I wrote no verse. Firstly I should say, because what remained of this impulse found relief in the writing of prose; and again, because the particular concentration, the state of feeling which conceived this kind of poem came more rarely with maturity, possibly because at all times it was a difficult world to live in, and I was no longer prepared to live in it. Certainly this impulse now turns more readily into other channels in which to find, I will not say a completer gratification, but anyhow a more available form of it. It seems to me now, not to go more deeply into the matter, that when I wrote poetry, I was, as it were, hanging in the void, and these poems are my efforts to establish contact, indeed this need is the one thing the poems express, in 1912 as in 1925: and it is as true of the jokes as of some whose main function, I remember, when they were written, was to shock. They shocked me as much as they did some readers and reviewers. But I had the compensation of being the initiator of that assault. That these still shock me is a sufficient comment on their author at this moment, and because of it, my choice has had to be responsible. Yet some of these poems, which partly I should have liked to omit, do seem to me successful in their "genre," and so they are included, excessive as, at this date, they seem. I think this much apology is needed—but only this much. The now-self for the then-self to the speculative reader.

To me, "The Hymn of Hymns" is probably the most striking of all Rodker's poems.

> God damn Cosmoses—
> Eternities, infinities
> and all that galley.
>
> God damn
> white mushroomy flaccid

144

and smelling of old clothes
Man!
whether Homeric
or after
Dostoievski.
Born between excrements
in death returning:
Futile cunning Man
(By cunning overcoming the life-inertia.)
Attacking the stars
from eyes five feet above ground.

God damn
Woman:
mushroomy flaccid
and smelling of old clothes Woman!
Her heirs and assigns
for ever.

God damn
the purulent pestilential wind,
and the pullulating sea,
the eternal, infinite, cosmical, blue,
deep, unfathomed, boundless, free,
racing, wild, mysterious sea—
Its argus-eyed, winged and lanthorned dwellers.
And you, Walt.

God damn
and eternally destroy
the twilight labour of the waterworks,
where in the pumping-room
sure pistons work—
(satyriast's beautitude.)

God damn
the incredible tragedies of their geometric ponds
fringed by poplars.

God damn streets
whose dust sends up syph and flu,
diarrhea and smallpox:
whose mean houses hold mean lives,
wallpaper, flypaper,
paperfaced brats.

God be with you, Reader.

To some he seemed too much a poet of despair. Yet, such is the sincerity and individualism in these poems that one's conviction is reaffirmed that even utter blackness may be a thing of beauty. The critic of the *Times* caught something of this in his review: "His are highly sensitised experiments in forms designed to represent his very unique reaction to the world. He sees that world rather pathologically, but is thereby only the more representative of the modern, nerve-wracked generation. . . . There is in almost all of these poems a particular, even a frenzied concentration of feeling."

Henry Crowder

Henry-Music

In the summer of 1930, I turned over the management of the Hours Press to Mrs. Wyn Henderson and her able young printer, John Sibthorpe, and left with Henry Crowder for southwest France where Henry planned to set several poems to music for the book to be called *Henry-Music*. I advanced Mrs. Henderson £300 to publish a short story by Richard Aldington, and three volumes of poetry by Harold Acton, Brian Howard, and Bob Brown. In addition, she and John printed the well-planned little catalogue of Hours Press books called *The Hours Press Booklet*, which has been invaluable in writing this book.

The pace had become arduous and hectic in the Rue Guenégaud as business grew and the rhythm of production increased. And I was learning that operating a press simply could not be handled alone, or almost alone. Yet it was not so bad as the "driven work"—Henry's words to me for what had gone on previously at Réanville. But we were glad to leave for a holiday in August, as soon as the last copy of Roy Campbell's poems had been packed and sent off. We drove south very fast in Henry's small dark blue car, the "Bullet," with scarlet lining, through panting, sun-scorched France, even as far as the confines of Pyrenean Andorra, on our search for shade and green fields. But nothing seemed right till we retraced our way a little and found the Dordogne river rolling like a great symphony in blue and green. Installing ourselves first at the inn in the then half-crumbling village of Creysse, and then in two rooms that might not have been inhabited for fifty years, we lived like the peasants, drawing water from a nearby fountain, and cooking of an evening by candlelight. The dear little place cost about £1 for one month. This is where the music was going to be written. Rough boards, full of what Henry called "air-holes," great heat, and the simple life go well together, but to the villagers we were totally inexplicable: one, a tall, imposing, handsome man of color, beautifully dressed, who spoke very little French; the other, an obvious English woman for all her Parisian accent and vocabulary. There was even the moment when, driving in the car through market day at Gramat, a driver, as if concerned with a pair of oxen, exclaimed on seeing us: "*Té! Ils ne sont pas de la même couleur!*" Why, said they, should we have chosen Creysse and not elsewhere? To reply, "It is so lovely here on the Dordogne," did not fully satisfy them. What could we be doing?

They soon heard. For the speed with which a small upright piano was hired from the little town of Martel nearby was remarkable. It arrived in an open farm-cart drawn by two beautiful oxen and was somehow hoisted up the narrow old stone stair into the cottage. Thus began the composing of *Henry-Music*, which continued daily, myself much in the fields with some writing, and in the river itself. In time the peasants saw us as "*des intellectuels étrangers*" and ceased wondering.

Henry Crowder, as I have said, was a handsome Afro-American of mixed Red Indian and African blood. He had

148

been born in Gainsville, Georgia, in 1895, the youngest
of the twelve children of a tanner. Almost from the start
of my press, he had been associated with the Hours, and
had learned to do well many chores connected with
printing. Like so many colored American musicians, he
had achieved his high level of execution as a pianist
through his own innate musicianship rather than by
academic study. He said he had always played, since he
was a child; "it just came natural." But he could also read
the most difficult scores, which, as everyone conversant
with jazz will know, is by no means the case with many
musicians of the kind who play by ear and instinct, by
memory and improvisation, all remarkably bound up
together.

These songs were Henry Crowder's first written and
published compositions. Many times as I listened to him
improvise on the piano at Réanville it seemed to me that
such musical thoughts and original harmonies and pro-
gressions should be set down. Why not a music book—
songs with words—published by the Hours? Henry's
modesty stood in the way of this for a while. But as I continued my pleading, he said he thought he could write
the music if lyrics and poems were found that seemed
to his purpose. And more improvisations flowed. Which
should come first—words or music? Immaterial, said he.
But no, on second thought, the words should be first. So
we began to look for poems that would inspire, and thus
I wrote a sort of battle hymn, called "Equatorial Way,"
in which the Negro says a fierce farewell to the United
States, and heads for an Africa that should be his. This was
not, as it may sound, out of sympathy for the movement
known as Garveyism, from its founder Marcus Garvey,
the Jamaican, who held that all the fifteen million or so

people of African and mixed descent in the United States should go back factually to Africa—but merely dictated by the romantic thought of the black man's return to the "Dark Continent."

Samuel Beckett, Richard Aldington, Harold Acton, and Walter Lowenfels all much appreciated Henry as a man and musician and gladly told him to choose from their poems. Such is *Henry-Music*, a small collection of six pieces that are quite different from each other in character. One of them is a "Blues" by me (with the Boeuf-sur-le-Toit cabaret in mind), which Henry used to sing there at times and in the other nightclubs where he played in the Paris of 1930 and 1931. It was recorded by Sonabel, but alas not well.

We had brought along the poems Henry had selected and subtle indeed were the harmonies that poured forth or were more slowly worked out and which, to my mind, are admirable for Samuel Beckett's poem and the "Creed" of Walter Lowenfels. Perhaps the music to Harold Acton's "Tiresias" is the most moving. The Aldington lyric is a lighter, pretty little piece.

The nights were velvet-dark and hot, with an old village woman forever washing loads of linen in a great ancient copper outside, the sparks pricking nightlong out of the wood beneath it, and Henry's hands going over his compositions as long as we thought permissible. Nearly everything was written here in the course of four weeks, so that we went back to Paris with the Opus almost finished. Creysse, said Henry, had been an inspiration. The great river was like a symphony of old, so old that perhaps it had never been written down, for it belonged to the times of primitive man when the prehistoric animals roamed this part of the earth and were limned in color some

20,000 years ago, in the caves of Les Eyzies, not so very far away, by artists as fine as any that ever lived. It is near here that I live today.

To find covers for *Henry-Music* was no problem. They should be reproductions of the African sculptures and carvings of which I by then had many. To do the covers Man Ray's name came to me at once, for he had not only a strong appreciation for African art but for Henry as well. I had known Man Ray and had admired his work for several years, probably since 1923 when my mother, who was most enthusiastic about his portraits, asked him to come to Dieppe, where I was also staying at the time, to photograph a prominent French banking family. Man Ray seldom spoke, but when he did his talk became concentrated and intense. He could speak brilliantly about photography as well as painting. I do not recall ever seeing one of his paintings. I remember only his great knowledge and control as a photographer, and I think he is a very great artist indeed.

Surely one of the most striking developments in the arts of the twenties is photomontage, and of course Man Ray had worked for years already as a photographer and montagiste. His vision in taking and placing and, as it were, in "mating" various objects, was often supreme. I think the many African ivory bracelets of considerable age, and the other pieces so beautifully set together by him on the two covers of *Henry-Music* are another proof of this. At the back of Henry's fine full face on the front cover is what looks like a sort of high collar—in reality my arms laden entirely with dozens of thin, disclike old ivory bracelets from West Africa. Had these covers, reproduced in black and white, been in color, they would have been even finer, on account of the generously rich scale of tones in African wood and ivory, so vibrant when seen at close range.

I had absorbed with interest and indignation Henry's accounts of the horrible strife between black and white in the United States, but it was not this alone which lead me to make my *Negro Anthology*, although Henry's many, ever fair-minded narrations were possibly the first cause. Of the accomplishments of the Negro and colored people there was also much to be written. I had read a good deal of Afro-American literature by now, and also loved all the various forms of jazz, which was the origin of my own small effort at a rather sophisticated "Blues," to which Henry wrote the music and sang with all the nostalgia the words imply:

> Back again between the odds and ends,
> Back again between the odds and ends,
> What once was gay's now sad,
> What was unknown's now friends.
>
> Each capital's not more than one cafe
> Wherein you lose, wherein you lose
> Yourself in what you have and have had,
> Why worry choose, why worry choose?
>
> The waiter waits, he will wait all night,
> And when you're tight he will set you right
> Back in tomorrow, or even yesterday . . .
> Time plays the piper, but what do we pay?
>
> Oh Boeuf-sur-le-Toit, you had one song,
> But when I look in the mirrors it all goes
>   wrong—
> Memory Blues, and only back today . . .
>   I'm a miserable travelling man.

HOURS PRESS
¹5, *Rue Guénégaud,* ¹5
PARIS 6ᵉ

A set of six Piano Pieces :

HENRY-MUSIC

by

HENRY CROWDER

with poems by

RICHARD ALDINGTON - HAROLD ACTON
NANCY CUNARD - WALTER LOWENFELS
SAMUEL BECKETT

in photographic covers on boards from a
series of photographs by Man Ray.
100 signed copies at 10 shillings.

This is the first published work of Mr Henry
Crowder. The reproductions on the covers
were made from African sculptures and ivories
in a private collection.

. *Ready November*

Henry–Music announcement

Henry Crowder

Perhaps among his many friends at this time, Samuel Beckett was the one who most appreciated Henry's charm and who greatly liked to hear him play. This is his poem that came out in *Henry-Music*.

FROM THE ONLY POET TO A SHINING WHORE
For Henry Crowder to Sing

Rahab of the Holy Battlements,
bright dripping shaft
in the bright bright patient
pearl-brow dawn-dusk lover of the sun.

Puttanina mia!
You hid them happy in the high flax,
pale before the fords
of Jordan, and the dry red waters,
and you lowered a pledge
of scarlet hemp.

Oh radiant, oh angry, oh Beatrice,
she foul with the victory
of the bloodless fingers
and proud, and you, Beatrice, mother, sister,
    daughter, beloved,
fierce pale flame
of doubt, and God's sorrow,
and my sorrow.

Richard Aldington

Last Straws

One characteristic of Richard Aldington about this time was the increasing contrast between the gay, friendly, good-natured side of him, plus his charming enthusiasm—all apparent and delightful with people he liked—and the angry, denunciatory, bitter mood, and the criticism of so much which had begun to appear in some of his work, though he had not yet reached the stage which prompted him, many years later, to write the very disagreeably false book that gives such a wrong impression and misrepresentative picture of Norman Douglas.

At the time of the publication of *Last Straws*, Aldington was somewhere quite far from Paris—it may have been in Florence—and I had not seen him, I think for quite a while. The story had been promised some months before. One supposed that he had been pleased with the great success his war novel, *Death of a Hero*, had earned him. His angry moods, as far as myself and various mutual friends were concerned, had not come our way; they went, rather, into some of his work. Critical he was, indeed (but so were many of us), of the acute despondency and blackness in outlook of the intellectuals about in Montparnasse, and I believe he liked and got on so well with Henry Crowder on account of the Afro-American's fresh and uninhibited view of life. On and off in Paris throughout the year, we had often been together with other poets and artists. It was of passing life we would mainly talk, of the complex nature of France and the peculiarities of the French.

One afternoon in particular remains in memory when the three of us sat in the Café d'Harcourt on the Boulevard St. Michel. Three gin fizzes were ordered, but when they came and had been tasted all three of us put down our glasses in consternation. An acrimonious argument with the waiter ensued. What else could it be but the best gin?, said he. Of course it was English gin, not a French brand, no one else had ever complained, and drink it or pay for it we certainly must. The manager of the café was called and went to fetch the bottle. And here was the explanation. The label said the contents were American gin. And of course the United States was dry at this time. Yet the Prohibition "hootch" racket seemed to have been running so well that the appalling stuff was actually being exported to unwary France.

The small episode made such an impression on Aldington that it got, through his account of it, into very many newspapers, as I could soon judge by the great number of clippings about it that my press-cutting agency sent to the Hours Press. Everyone seemed to have read of the incident and this little press fanfare caused someone to remark that he certainly knew how to look after his publicity as an author.

The remark may have been dictated by jealousy, for his name was very much to the fore at this time and advance notices were coming out about now of his translation of *Fifty Romance Lyric Poems* and a new novel, *The Colonel's Daughter*, which were to appear fairly soon.

People wanted to read what he wrote and this was evident to me for a few weeks preceding the publication of *Last Straws*. The two book travellers I now had—Mr. Gray, mainly for London, and Mr. Dracott, for the provinces—sent in a most gratifying number of advance orders. With the exception of Norman Douglas's *One Day*, which also came out in two editions of two hundred and three hundred each, no other book of the Hours ran to a total of five hundred copies. Almost all were sold before publication day in December.

At this time, as temporary manager of the Hours Press, Mrs. Henderson had the choosing of the binding of both editions and brought them out very well, the signed one bound in jade green suede cloth boards with gilt lettering, the other edition in charming light brown paper boards with designs on them by Douglas Cockerell.

I cannot recall if Aldington told me anything about when he wrote this story. Possibly he had done so shortly before it was published, or it may have been some time before. One can argue that such a postwar mood might have been more in touch with the rhythm of Europe as it was around 1918. By 1930 much that was new had come up everywhere. And yet, disgust with life (apart from that connected with the conduct of someone lately beloved, which is the main reason for the disgust of one of the three characters) may come upon people long after the sound of the firing has gone, and be connected with it all the same, and with what has followed. Of course he had been through World War I as a soldier, and, like nearly everyone, was disappointed and indignant at feeling it had probably been no kind of war to put an end to further wars, a realization that had diverse effects on various people, some of whom brooded and despaired, others attempted more or less successfully to get away from war psychosis and its aftereffects, and turn to the new trends, hopes, and experiments that existed in the manifestations of art and intellect.

Last Straws is a bitter story of three Englishmen who, while not very much more than "average" people in most ways, are at least lucid enough—for all the nightclub atmosphere around their conversation—to discuss the war they have been through and the deplorable aftertaste it has left in the world. This they start to do at first in one of those Paris nightclubs where physical ego and mental self are reduced by noise, boredom, and wine-fumes to vapidity and vacuity. Who doesn't know that mood? It ran with fluency down Aldington's pen, an excellent implement for spleen. Moreover, although the story upset several of the critics, it was convincingly written; it was meant to be bitter, and bitter it was. What is wrong with that? I suppose it was thought to be exaggerated, too cynical. And yet, what occurs at the end—when one of the three disgruntled ex-officers goes back to England and shoots his wife's lover and himself—must have happened often enough in real life.

The critic of the *London Mercury* was one who found *Last Straws* disappointing. "It is a pity," he wrote, "that a writer of Mr. Aldington's reputation should put his name to this story, for there is nothing to be said in favor of *Last Straws*, either in the context or in the writing. The conversation of three drunken men at a night club is hardly worth recording and the end is pure melodrama." But the *Observer* reviewer found it "a sad and bitter story, with real character drawing and atmosphere. The action passes in Paris and the characters are suffering the nervous afterstrain of the war."

And now occurred something between Aldington and me that left me completely baffled as to the reason of it. Since both editions of *Last Straws* were selling well, why not send him some advance royalties? Off went a cheque from the temporary manager, which to my surprise came back with an angry letter saying that the story had been *given me* to publish and not to the manager. "But the royalties are from the Press," I pointed out in reply; "What is the difference?" More expostulations followed, until a real row by correspondence ensued. How well I remember Norman Douglas's remark when told of this: "Why *do* authors have such difficulties with each other? I'm sure *grocers* don't behave that way among themselves!"

Harold Acton

This Chaos

The poems in *This Chaos*, so characteristic of their author as he was in the late twenties, show various facets of his interesting and attractive personality. There are also signs in them of what he was to develop into. Although already cultured in his youth, he has become scholarly and erudite in middle age, and what was spontaneous and accomplished is now enriched by thoughtfulness and learning. The craftsmanship of these poems (I thought then and still think now) was like his personal appearance— handsome and cut with a dash.

How often one has wondered what is meant exactly by the expression "of his time." An age will contain authors as different, say, as T. S. Eliot and Ernest Hemingway, yet both are distinctly representative, dominantly, if oppositely so. This representativeness is surely partly a thing of class and milieu as well as of *zeitgeist*. If, as in Acton's case, it begins at Eton and Oxford, Harold Acton and his contemporary and close friend in those days, Brian Howard (whose poems were published by the Hours immediately after *This Chaos*), were very much that side of the twenties. I mean that I think of them together as they were then in their early times, though they were certainly not anything like "a pair," or one complementing the other. Both were aesthetes, and how much more. For both there was the same kind of enquiring restlessness, set on and directed against the background of English ease, which they could all the same enjoy. They had revolt and a very good critical spirit, a zest for innovation, and excellent taste. Both were *jeunesse dorée*; good conversation, often sparkling and most original, was theirs, and both possessed quick minds, knowledge and perception of art. Though friends as well as rivals, they collaborated before their university days to bring out *The Eton Candle* (bound in bright, arresting pink), a collection of contemporary poetry and prose which, along with art and literary reviews, took an honorable place in the bookshops. If they sometimes tended to appear a trifle *précieux*, well, I cannot tell about that, for such was never the way I knew and liked them so well. They loved travel and, being internationally minded, they kept in touch with the intellectual personalities of Europe as well as England. Now and again they indulged in the "treasure hunt" currents of London. But how differently after those early years each developed.

Partly American and partly English-Italian, Acton— or at least one side of him—can be said, I suppose, to be "very Oxford" in tradition and education, yet not entirely so in upbringing, for his love of Italy (where he was born) and his innate response to it were always there. His heart is in Italy and small wonder; it was Florence that influenced him so much from the start. He lives there mainly at present, in the great palace of La Pietra, whose personality was created by his father, an art connoisseur and collector, who had a happy eye at the end of the last century for acquisitions, and who turned at least a score of rooms into veritable museums of ancient Italian art, beside making an exquisite garden. Naples, too, he lives in, working on at his monumental *History of the Bourbons of Naples*. There is also much of Chinese culture to him, for he has spent a number of years in China, writing, teaching, translating.

He could certainly be described as something of an intellectual dandy when I first knew him, for although serious-minded, he was also mundane, swift, gay, and full of sparkling, malicious shafts and arrows when occasion demanded. The words "easy, noiseless and rapid" (an echo of those days, but in what context?) were applicable to his buoyant personality, his way of moving about London and the Continent. If there was an up-to-dateness about him, there was also a thoroughness, and well is this proved by his evolution into the man of real culture, the excellent linguist, the beautiful lecturer with an exact technique. Today, he is still the sound friend he was, and the urbane, witty raconteur remains as lively and well informed.

Acton's contribution to my *Grand Man*, a very good reminiscence of Norman Douglas, shows how well he understood and appreciated the ways of that genial sage who was something of a mentor to him in Florence, where he had known him long. Douglas liked the finesse of Acton and had a flair as to where he would find life most congenial: in China. He encouraged Harold to go, and the poet's sojourn in China proved to be a turning point in his life. The poise and the urbaneness inherent in him were greatly developed by the surrounding Chinese rhythms, scholastically and otherwise. His *Peonies and Ponies*, written while in China, is an amusing, searching, and and ironical novel on European and Chinese characters, very different from his early aesthetic work, *Cornelian*, which he called "a fable in prose." In the happy and productive years prior to the Second World War, Harold taught, translated modern Chinese poetry, and studied the Chinese theater. But the war put an end to all this, and he joined the RAF.

Douglas was in Paris on a lengthy visit about the time *This Chaos* was to come out, that would be in the late autumn of 1930, and the two men went about often together, scholarly conversation alternating with the brusque, schoolboy sallies shot off by "Uncle Norman," who indulged, always unexpectedly, in such. At least once Harold got Norman to a source of "advanced art," although I don't think I ever managed to get him inside the Galerie Surréaliste. The place was André Breton's studio, which contained a striking collection of surrealist paintings. The scene has been amusingly recreated in Harold's enchanting *Memoirs of an Aesthete*. "After one horrified look at the Dali dominating Breton's room—an intricately demoniac picture of William Tell in his underwear with a bright phallus protruding, and such details as the carcass of a donkey on a piano with a horse galloping over it—Uncle Norman said sharply: 'I can't stay here. That picture will spoil my dinner. See you later. I must get some fresh air at once.'"

I find it still a little strange that Acton, who was so proficient in classic and oriental art, should have been somewhat bewildered by the art of the primitive peoples that adorned my shop in Rue Guenégaud. But, as already said, such sculptures in the early thirties were far less known and appreciated, although Epstein, Henry Moore, and a great many other artists liked them immensely. His reaction to Rue Guenégaud is most amusing.

Fetishes from Easter Island and the Congo held rendezvous among freshly printed poems. "What are we doing here?" they asked. "Let's

This Chaos

by

HAROLD ACTON

HOURS PRESS
15, Rue Guénégaud PARIS
1930

Title page from *This Chaos* by Harold Acton

run away . . ." They refused to stay put. They disturbed conversation with their antics and distracted one's thoughts. Each contained a separate universe. One expected them to march out of the door and up the street, shouting slogans in a truculent procession. On the whole I think they were kindly disposed to my poems. "Wait a while" I could hear one saying, a rascal from the Gold Coast in a permanent state of excitement, "I rather like this about Harold Acton in his bath."

His poems—dedicated to me—were being printed, I think, at that moment. *This Chaos* (a good title but certainly not applicable to the style of his well-written poetry, nor yet to that of his thoughts) is a collection of sixteen poems, in part lyrical, full of grace, and of feeling too; there is erudition in them, and also a sort of personal flourish, and a delicious playfulness. "Soap," "Razor," and "Narcissus to His Sponge" form a hygienic trilogy that is sprightly, delicate, and highly suggestive. "Aubade" completes the ritual of washing. The one called "Soap" had already appeared in *The London Mercury*, where, as its author says in the same *Memoirs*, "it attracted the editor of *Progress* (published by Lever Brothers in the interests of the company, its shareholders, customers, and staff), who wrote for permission to reproduce 'a poem which has, as you may imagine, a specific interest for us soapmakers.'" Sensuous and charming is the concluding image:

> Winter is caught in this wet web—
> A winter without winter's rage
> Where locks go white without old age;
> And in a basin I'll remember
> The ruffled ermine of a whole December.

Several of the poems are in this vein. Others, like "Tiresias" (also published in *Henry-Music*) are serene or tragic. "Blake" is very striking.

These Were the Hours

> I saw a poet in a wood
> And his body was an oak,
> And the sap that was his blood
> Twisting through the branches broke
> Into leaf so innocent
> That no-one knew what the hell it meant.
> And some dodderers arose
> Called him odd and called him quaint;
> Age asserted—He's a seer;
> Youth—he is a mighty saint.
> Saint and seer, and quaint and odd,
> Why not call the poet God?

The production of *This Chaos* was pleasing. Its covers, specially designed by that excellent painter, Elliott Seabrooke, who also designed the cover for my own volume of poems, *Poems (Two) 1925*, issued by Aquila Press at the same time, were described by Harold Acton as "the jagged blue on white collarbone of a hare." Unfortunately, not one review of the book is left.

168

Brian Howard

First Poems

Were one word only allowed to describe the poems in this volume the word that comes to me is "intensity." Luckily there is no such rule, and other words may be added: passion of feeling; highly individual modulations from one thought to another, from one image to the next; a personal and rather new sense of language; compression of ideas; a fine ear; and an often surging line. But I must always return to the first word, "intensity." Next I fall to thinking that those who had an affinity with this kind of poetry thirty years ago (but was there much of it in any case?) would find that these poems are not so very far from today.

In some ways Brian Howard was one of the *poètes maudits* of eternity. The stamp of this is on his poems, and, to a great extent, for one reason or another—mainly emotive ones—it was on his life. Unfortunately he has not written very much poetry, and, of course, "the restlessness of the born poet" (as who has said?) was not his only characteristic, although I think that from the way he felt about life and the way he expressed himself it was the dominant one. For all his creative nervous energy and enthusiasm, his admirable sense of humor and exuberance, his resilience, his capacity for working things out,

169

too, there seemed to be often a contrary fate about him, a something as if "for ever on the way," with what fluctuations between optimism and despondency. It could be said of him that he had his head in the clouds and his feet on the ground. Yet it was the clouds that eventually claimed him to themselves. On account of his sometimes terrific "panache" (it was the permanent *jeunesse dorée* side of him), of his frequently biting tongue, fits of wild generosity and also of self-indulgence, his teasings and tauntings, many thought him entirely too "extreme." But his friends were devoted and long-proven. Personally, I, who knew him very well for many years, appreciated his hypersensivity (always very clear to me) in his emotion about life as it passed, now beautifully, now hideously. His mockery and his elegant irony were so many buttresses, and they enchanted me. He was self-dramatizing and, indeed, self-consuming; the pendulum swung far and wide. I suppose he was very much of his time (again that expression mystifies me), but his appearance seemed to me so romantic that it belonged rather to a previous age, being also as little that of a typical Anglo-Saxon as of the twentieth century. His dark handsomeness was Latin, with something Spanish to the long, lean figure, to the gaze of the eyes that could become so intense and acute, to the enthusiastic gesture, the sometimes apostrophising attitude.

It was by stages we got to know each other so well, first during the war at many a party in London, then in the twenties in the evening cafés and cabarets of Paris; in other places too, up in the snows one winter at Obergurgl, in Austria, where I travelled with Henry to try skiing; at my house at Réanville during the summer of 1937 when the idea came to me (and was encouraged by him) of addressing the *Enquête* on the Spanish War to the writers of Britain. He wrote a beautiful sonnet, "For Those with Investments in Spain," which I set by hand and published in my series of *plaquettes* sold for Spanish Republican relief that year. Yet, knowing him, even at the start, was to feel we had always known each other. The first contact must have been over *The Eton Candle* (edited by him and Harold Acton while still at Eton) in the mid-twenties. The great friendship and understanding of each other came into being about the time I published his *First Poems*. To me they reflect amazingly his particular extremes; exaltation and exultation are here, but not those of happiness; there is a sense of tragedy about them, the ring of them is most true to himself.

Brian Howard was "an exotic" from the very start of his iridescent youth at Eton and Oxford, up till the moment of his untimely death in 1958. In all the avatars produced by his extravagant temperament, at grips in his latter years with lengthy physical illness and psychic *wanderlust*, there was always the element of extraordinariness. He was never macabre; he was most sane, but how often dominated by fantasy—literally dominated. He had the faults of some of his qualities: he could be intensely kind, appreciative, generous, and his exuberance, his violence, even, of heart could overflow, and then he could set to work all attired in arrogance and provocativeness. His sharp likes could vie with his trenchant hatreds, and his often very outspoken contempt for fools and the second-rate earned him many an enemy, whose least word against him might be "dilettante." How his personality could swing about on occasion. Its foundations, however, were on solid and rich ground. He was extremely civilized and had beautiful breeding and taste in art and culture of all sorts, in architecture, in dress, in food. He was a fine talker and a very witty narrator, excellent at description, knowing well where to lay an emphasis, how to heighten his caricature. To this add the gift of repartee, and an admirable reading voice. And he also seemed to *understand* everything about those he really liked or loved.

There was quite another side to him too—I mean to that of his "artistic temperament"—for he could set himself to work at regular things such as literary criticism and journalism and wrote some very analytical book reviews for the *New Statesman*. And through having means enough he could travel for pleasure, and as the years passed his travel increased. When I first knew him his interest had already been for Germany and Austria, but when things began to look ugly there in the early thirties, his desire to know what was going on became more and more thorough. He detested fascism in all its forms, and stayed in touch with many of the intellectuals and others there who shook their heads over the rise of Hitler. For some years he made long stays in what was becoming, and had become, the realm of the Swastika. His active brain and good mind, his reading, his perceptiveness, his sympathy and concern for the youth of Germany that was being indoctrinated with lies produced some very clearly reasoned descriptions, and also a spate of denunciation of the facts he had been living amidst. How was it that, each time he returned to England, or even to France, not enough people cared nor wanted to be made aware of the hideous import of these facts, these obviously lucid indications? Why, save for a minimum of really politically minded people, were they, seemingly, not even interested? *Must* one be politically minded to be concerned at the appalling things going on? What about being merely human? How often he would movingly talk to me thus.

His approach to facts was very realistic, his reactions were certainly on the simple human plane, which is the most honest one, and by then he had a good deal of personal knowledge of those countries to back up all he said. His German was excellent and he was certainly familiar with the psychology and ways of thinking of the Germans; his years among them and the Austrians had given him that. If only his description of the very end of Munich week in 1938, after all the statesmen had flown away again, had been taken down as narrated, there would be on record a pretty historical asterisk. It was symbolical, somehow. After all the frantic fear and tension there, he had come upon two old English aristocrats (a man and his wife who were thoroughly unconcerned with Hitlerian matters), both on their knees by a sofa in the lounge of a hotel where so much that was portentous had been debated. What were they doing? Hunting pitifully, if querulously, for a lost knitting needle.

Small wonder that, back in England during World War II, he should have been so angry at things like this said to him by fellow officials: "How can that German be the horrible Nazi you say? Why, the man was at Eton with me!" Before the war ended Brian served in the ranks of one of the ground crews of the R.A.F.

A Spanish musician once said to me: "What is an artist? A being within whose hands life quivers and vibrates." It seems to me this could be well said of Brian Howard. It is unfortunate that he did not write much more poetry, yet, even so, because of what exists, it is ever as the poet I think of him; the stress is on that. So this quotation from his lengthy poem "God Save the King" (the volume published by me was to have been called that in the first

place) is as long as possible. As far as I know his poems have
not been reprinted in book form, but they certainly
should be.

Under the sailing cedar tree, in a heavy August
the elders sat on the lawn, eating a little tea.
The sun was in the silver, and the blue cuckoo, the bird
    Ophelia
spoke her pure word, down in the field,
spoke and spoke again, words of virginal madness.
Mother dwindled towards the vegetables
and grew back to us again, leaning through the afternoon,
    a daisy on a tide,
a bottle of milk in a green afternoon.

But, as dirt gets between the teeth, and sweat creeps
    between the piano keys,
worms into everyone, nails into a cross,
so Mars, the loud newspaper boy, rode across our roses
and trampled our teacups into the lawn.
No storm-scene destroyed our pastoral symphony,
    no grand tempest, but instead
as dirt gets into the teeth, the newspaper got in at the
    garden gate
and we were all filled with hate.
It wasn't for want of wishing, of waiting and watching . . .
    ah no,
we were always awfully careful, even at Oddenino.
Black dirt, white dirt, all on a printed page,
    we didn't *believe* you
because of Cambridge Cornwall, vows in a punt,
because we were being *young* so *beau*tifully.

Mother returned from the vegetables, on the run through
   the ruins of the minute,
sat on a garden chair and thrust her roots down among
   the daisies
in search of an older strength.
Father cursed, and Ophelia fell from the bough
snapping a Flanders poppy where she fell.
Father's age, too old, made itself into a monument beside
   Mother,
an evening monument, and the eyelids were a little weary.
We went. We left by the evening train, never again.

The covers of *First Poems* were especially designed by
the well-known painter, John Banting, best friend to
Brian Howard nearly all of his life, and beautiful they are,
executed in large block letters in a striking sort of false
perspective, with indications of small branches in between,
printed in dull red on duck's-egg blue paper boards.

The only review of *First Poems* that I have is by Alan
Pryce Jones, in *The London Mercury*, a perceptive and
intelligent commentary well worth quoting.

I do not mean to disparage Mr. Howard's poetry, when I say it is
essentially of our age—as easily dated as Cowley or Monckton
Milnes, or T. S. Eliot. It has the extreme sensitiveness to external
impressions, the pride, and a sort of anguish at being alive at all,
which are usually the springs of modern inspiration. Just as sleepless-
ness often attacks everyone in a house together, visions of collapse
overshadow the arts. The disruption of our times has cracked the face
of nature.

O Life!
Bend down, bend my bow, send my arrow high, now, not low,
   below.

These Were the Hours

I am my arrow. I have thick hearts to kill, that have killed me.
   Yet, I am.
I, still, am. Hurl me hard, high, and I will kill, and live,
   and still give life, O Life.

This is the poetry of defence. Mr. Howard takes his philosophy
from Germany rather than from France—it must be granted that
the philosophy, the spark, of any poetic renewal comes to us from
one or the other; perhaps that in all times and countries radical
changes in artistic outlook have come violently in from abroad—
and he is on the whole pessimistic. But the philosophy of poetry
ought not to be an integral part of poetry, but a screen for poetry to
play against; so it is more important to say that Mr. Howard, except
when the hard brilliance of his style rarely glitters without
illuminating, writes extremely well:

Stand, figure! Stand upon the future, while the past
   and the present drop, nails
   from your high hands and feet.
Stand, figure, and live, and live! While the future
   swings and blazes upon the only landscape.
   The new sun roars above. It is all the birds.
Stand, figure! All the flowers burst and roll upon the rocks.
It is the end. The heart is building. It is the beginning.

Bob Brown

Words

The author of *Words* was a lively minded American, then about forty years old, who seemed to me both phenomenal and at the very center of his time, a *zeitgeist* in himself. I think we must have got in touch when he sent me a copy of his *1450–1950* (the title refers to the evolution of printing), which was beautifully produced in 1929 by Caresse Crosby at her Black Sun Press in Paris. True, the surrealists had been experimenting for some years in reshaping writing, and so had the dadaists before them, and E. E. Cummings and other Americans had loosed some entirely novel currents in the general stream of poetry, but the forthright, individual thoughts and speculations of Bob Brown had yet another new slant. The arrangement of his words and simple line drawings in this volume were admirably blended and the layout was charming. Here was no tongue-in-cheek, as you might think at first look, but the pristine *joie-de-vivre*, full of shafts such as,

> Ho! Ho!
> How can you
> Get anything at all
> In this life
> Without throwing

177

Both your arms
And both your legs
Around it?

One critic called *1450–1950* "an excellent symbol of what symbolism is trying to do."

When I had met and known Bob Brown a little, in Paris and Cagnes-sur-Mer, where Kay Boyle, George Antheil, Hilaire Hiler, and Harry and Caresse Crosby resided for a while, it seemed to me that these lines could be the very motto of his life, which comprised such a diversity of things grasped, enjoyed, and developed to the full. He was certainly a persistent experimenter, forever in and out of felicitous discoveries, intoxicated by words, yet knowing how to bring them to heel.

He had recently come to Paris when we first met, was rightly accounted one of the "moderns" and was a friend of, or in touch with, all the well-known American expatriates—Ezra Pound, Gertrude Stein, Sylvia Beach, Eugene Jolas, Walter Lowenfels, William Bird, Robert McAlmon, and how many more.

Brown had travelled in many countries, and I remember the sort of aura of "practised traveller" there was to him, and the impression he made on me of an interesting blend of straightforward astuteness, gaiety, and hospitality. If he and his enchanting wife, Rose, were constantly moving about, they seemed to settle for a time profitably wherever they had a mind to.

Before his arrival in France he had been a journalist and had become famous as a writer of thrillers in the United States under the name of Robert Carlton Brown. Along with the publication of many stories in popular magazines, poems of his appeared in American literary reviews. As a fiction editor for a time, he did much freelancing, and actually wrote and sold 1,000 short stories in ten years. He once owned three commercial newspapers at the same time, in Rio de Janeiro, Mexico, and London, collected jade in China, and loved antiques and ethnography. He once lived in Japan and then in London, Montparnasse, and Cagnes-sur-Mer, and it was in the last named that he published his anthology *Readies* (1931), made for a strange experiment—no less than the construction and marketing of a Reading-Machine.

Another deft idea was Brown's attack on censorship entitled *Gems: A Censored Anthology*, which he dedicated to me in hopes that I would find it "a lifelong fountain of innocent and exalted pleasure." Bob's technique was to quote passages from many well-known poems considered classics and then, by imposing a blank over three or four words in each poem, to arouse the thought that censorship is apt to make all sorts of innocent things look pornographic. Here are a few excerpts.

Mother Goose jingles lend themselves superbly to the censor's purposes. A little book of familiar nursery rhymes appeared in America a few years ago; the classical verses were most improperly clothed in dashes, modern fig-leaves, accurately accenting and properly pointing the latent impropriety of such gems as:

> Old Mother Goose, when
> She wanted to ★ ★ ★
> Would ★ ★ ★ a fat goose
> Or a very fine gander.

And Goldsmith and Wordsworth seemed just as cooperative as Mother Goose:

These Were the Hours

> Near yonder copse where once ★ ★ ★
> And still where many a ★ ★ ★ grows wild;
> There, where a few torn shrubs the place disclose.
> The village preacher's modest ★ ★ ★ rose.

.　　.　　.　　.　　.

> My ★ ★ ★ leaps up when I behold
> A ★ ★ ★ in the ★ ★ ★:
> So was it when my ★ ★ ★ began,
> So is it now I am a man,
> So be it when I shall grow old
> Or let me die!

The diversity of his life is reflected in many of his poems and writings, whose far-flung thoughts are in keeping with his particular dynamism. Everything about him had zest and this remained true until his death in New York, in 1959, not very long after he had revived the Roving Eye Press. Obviously such a man will have the most liberal and progressive ideas and feelings about life, yet not all who are thus are by any means prepared to do active things in the field of human concerns. There was a time (I think it was during the winter of 1935 and the year or two that followed) when he and his wife settled in one of the southern states of the U.S., in Arkansas, and were active there (was it not at Mena?) with a school. It may have been an entirely new school founded by them. What is certain is that it encouraged co-education of white and colored students, and there was a great outcry from various state authorities; this was somewhat attenuated later owing to the protests sent by European personalities against the barbaric custom of segregation. Here at this time Bob

Brown also founded and ran a lively college magazine.

After that we lost sight of each other. Throughout World War II, Bob and his wife worked part of the time for the Cultural Department of the U.S. Government, founding the Ecuatorian-American Cultural Club in Quito. And then quite recently I learned he was directing the Roving Eye Press in New York, from which came the following notice: "We take pride in reuniting this pair (Walter Lowenfels and Bob Brown) three decades after their Paris days when Nancy Cunard published Lowenfels's *Apollinaire* in 1930 and Bob Brown's *Words* in 1931, the same year they appeared together in *Readies for Bob Brown's Machine*. To last this long a creator in words has to be good."

The Roving Eye Press was not a new name, for he had started it in Cagnes in 1931, and it published that fantastic anthology, *Readies*, to which I contributed a condensed poem. *Readies* contains some of the wildest flights of verse and prose of that time by many impressive contributors like Alfred Kreymborg, Eugene Jolas, Ezra Pound, Gertrude Stein, James T. Farrell, Kay Boyle, Lawrence Vail, Paul Bowles, Robert McAlmon, Samuel Putnam, Walter Lowenfels, and William Carlos Williams. Included in the substantial volume is a businesslike photograph of the Reading-Machine, and it certainly appears to be more than a mere gadget. Its purpose was to increase one's reading speed by sending a tape containing the words across an 8 inch opening where the reader could see it. The reader would keep his eyes straight ahead and regulate the speed of the tape to suit himself. Whatever one may think of this, it must be said that all of us who responded to Bob's request for an "experimental piece of writing to suggest as novel a departure from the book as the talkies compared to the stage" were aware that writing must also be speeded up by abbreviation. The results promised to be startling.

An American journalist called the project "the latest quiverings of the avant-garde. Bob Brown offers the world a Reading-Machine—a new idea, he played with it for 15 years and now it pops without ceremony. It functions like a Wall Street ticker, words are to be printed in microscopic type on a winding spool of tape and read under a strong glass. Books will no longer be necessary, and 100,000 words may be concealed in a hollow tooth. Bob hopes with this process to speed up reading. If only he could speed up the human brain, the machine would be a wow." Looking again now into *Readies*, where, as the critic said, "unnecessary words are deleted and punctuation has been reformed to suit the instrument," one realized that speeding up does not mean anything so lucidly simple as telegraphese. Far from it!

Bob Brown was possessed by the thought of print and words. How right then it is that his Hours Press volume should be called *Words* and carry the subtitle, "I but bend my finger in a beckon, and words, birds and words, hop on chirping." It is dedicated "To my Rose-Rib," his wife. My hope for the binding had been a reproduction of a large slab of old ivory, the veining standing out dark on the printed surface. This turned out to be too difficult; the reproduction would not have been sharp enough. So the covers are cream paper boards with a red leather spine, in my usual poetry format. The front one bears the title, author's name and press imprint, in wonderfully intricate, well-planned formations of type, thanks to the imagination and skill of John Sibthorpe, who was obviously in sympathy with Bob Brown's poems and his love of printed letters. The cover is a cascade of type.

The poet had long been incubating his plan for the Reading-Machine and it was now very near actual birth. A preview of *Words* (in the Paris edition of the *Herald Tribune*, Dec. 26, 1929) said that this volume would "contain an essay in printing which Bob Brown later hopes to develop for a mechanical reading apparatus. But this machine is another notion of his and it must be described in another treatise, although Brown would not object to poetry and machinery being garbled up in the same story, for he sees poetry in machinery. The essay on printing in the forthcoming volume will be thus: the body of the text will be in 16 point type, set slightly to one side of the page; in one corner the same text will be found in microscopic type. The reader will be able to choose which he prefers, his action depending on the strength of the magnifying glasses at hand." The idea found expression in the following squib:

> In the reading-machine future
> Say by 1950
> All magnum opuses
> Will be etched on the
> Heads of pins
> Not retched into
> Three volume classics
> By pin heads

This preview is an excellent example of what one plans to do and how circumstances can alter the idea. Many attempts were made to get really microscopic type; it would be "great fun to do this" is what we said. But the right kind of type—it could hardly have been even 1-point —was not available, and even if it had been we could not be sure that these fly-speck letters would come out on the strong, thick paper. So the pieces of "microscopery" that look like tiny seals were printed from specially engraved plates on a lighter, smoother paper. A sample one, a mere breath of print on the page, but an eighth of an inch square when peered at through a strong glass, is just, just readable, and the one in question reveals this.

> Writing with a
> Fountain pen
> Is dull work
> Gimme a regular pen
> Or a fountain

All such little midgets may be thought of as asterisks to each poem in 16-point, and yet they are *not*, as had first been planned, any part of the poem, but items in their own right.

This poem in *Words* contains much of the "Bob Brown spirit" as well as his characteristic rhythm:

LAMENT OF AN ETCHER

> I have etched and etched
> Scratched a thousand
> Coppers, zincs and alloys
> Filled them with criss-crosses
> Zig-zags and cross-hatches
> Like finely woven spider-webs
> I might have spent my time
> To more purpose
> Weaving panama hats
> For all the public cares
> About real Art
> And now

Old and broken
Unappreciated
In spite of my exhausting effort
To make the Brooklyn Bridge
Look true to life
As accurate as a photograph
With every cable stretched and taut and
All the finely scratched little lines
Just as God put them in our thumbs
I face failure and renounce
The unappreciative public
In future I will devote myself to
An even subtler Art
From this day onward
I will scratch my back
For my own exclusive pleasure
Scratch it and scratch it
Backwards and forwards
This way and that
With an old yellow-fingered
Chinese ivory back-scratcher
Shaped as a long-nailed
Grasping ghostly hand
With all my skill
I will scratch
As finely as the finest etching
Grave with supreme technique
Superb sworling compositions
On my back where even I
Cannot see my masterpieces
My art shall henceforth be
Concealed from all
Art for Art's sake.

Havelock Ellis

The Revaluation of Obscenity

This book, the last volume to appear under the imprint of the Hours Press before it closed down, was produced entirely by Mrs Henderson, whose contract with me for running the press had now come to an end. At that moment I was lengthily in the south of France, working on my next project, the *Negro Anthology*, and the fact that Ellis's book appeared under the Hours Press imprint was a surprise even to me, for it had never figured on my list, nor had its publication been mentioned or discussed. However, its excellence and the fact that it was by this author, whom I esteemed greatly, were all to the good.

It is a beautiful piece of writing, the subject is soundly developed (one would not imagine anything written by the great savant to be otherwise) and it is erudite and flowing. The point is thoroughly made that the banning of works that come up against the courts is not only bad but frequently defeats its own supposed ends.

I met Havelock Ellis only once, on the occasion that I have mentioned when Arthur Symons brought him to dinner in an apartment I had on the Ile St. Louis in Paris. It was in 1926 and, although he was considerably older than Arthur Symons, there was a striking and beautiful vitality to him. Maybe that is what struck one first of all, and then something rhythmically harmonious in the poise, in the noble head and splendid, piercing eyes. There was also an aura of kindliness and serenity about him, a sort of quiet projection of the wisdom and knowledge within.

How many years before, towards the end of World War I, two or three of us were reading various parts of his magnificent *Studies in the Psychology of Sex*, already rare and difficult to procure. Reading aloud at times to each other, we marvelled at his great knowledge, at his calm approach to the facts and mysteries in nature. There, so interestingly described, were all these case histories, quirks, and peculiarities and habits sometimes conditioned by a way of life imposed by circumstances and not by choice; (at random I remember some remarkable passages about homosexuality among tramps in the U.S.A.). What educated person, normally healthy in mind, is going to find "salacious" or "obscene" such an honest set of studies written in such a masterly manner? Humanity, rich in emotive, romantic, and subjective values (thanks be), must also be seen and analyzed objectively. Interest in *all and any* of the facets and doings of human beings cannot be dismissed as a lewd thing; it is one part of anthropology —the study of the development of man. The *why* of this or that is fundamentally scientific since man began to *think*; the study of stone and insect, of star and psyche is also interlinked.

By the time Malinowski's *Sexual Life of Savages* came out, many years after the seven-volume work of Havelock Ellis, there was less prudery and fuss over writings on various aspects of human behavior. But it would be interesting if someone made a collection of the protests against censorship and banning stretching throughout history. To open Bob Brown's *Gems: A Censored Anthol-*

ogy, published in 1931, was to find some details (probably
forgotten now by most people) about how things went
when the first volumes of Ellis's monumental work
appeared. Here is what Brown wrote:

In a recent catalog an outspoken American rare-book dealer in
London publishes the following: "ELLIS (Havelock). Studies in The
Psychology of Sex, Vol. II, The Evolution of Modesty, The
Phenomena of Sexual Periodicity, Auto-Eroticism. Extremely fine.
8. Leipzig. The University Press, Limited, 1900." The English Court
put its foot down on the first volume. Proceedings of bestiality, cor-
ruption, lewdness, and all the classic formalism were hurled against
poor Havelock Ellis for daring to consent to write Volume I. The case
hung fire and finally in the summer of 1900, the book was officially
by State, Church, and Justice banned and prohibited—the publisher,
Mr. Geoffrey Mortimer, was determined to print Volume II in spite
of all the laws of heaven and earth, so his ruse was to print "Leipzig"
as the place of publication, believing that the cops wouldn't walk
to that place to burn up the stock. But the plan was too simple as
everything about the paper, type, etc. was English, and in spite of
Leipzig, the stock was seized and destroyed; I believe his plant was
near Cambridge. Then a few months later, F. A. Davis and Co. of
Philadelphia, consented to take over the publishing rights and have
been printing the rest of the series. Volume II is the rarest and most
precious of the 7 volumes. The first two volumes may only be sold to
Rabbis, Ministers, Parsons, Lawyers, librarians, and people over the
Climacteric and Menopause stages. Perhaps (it depends on the local
censor) students of Art, Love, Life and Literature may be able to buy
it with their own money, provided the local nurse says "yes" to the
purchaser. Mr. Ellis tells me this story. "I can't understand those
Americans. My *Psychology* is printed and sold in America and I try to
send a friend of mine in America a French edition of my *Studies* and
the licensed smut-hounds destroy it as obscene"—and he thought
(innocent soul) that I could answer him. I told him that was one of the
reasons I shook "God's Own Country." Things are easier in England.
All one does is this. A gentleman comes into a bookshop and wants
the set, and if the bookseller is wise he smiles and says, "You're a
Rabbi, aren't you?" (if the Patron's nose is outstanding). But if he is

just an ordinary Saxon he slips this bolony: "Oh yes, you're a man of God, surely you're a clergyman, dear brother in Christ," and if he says "No" the deal is off—but if he is at all intelligent he says "Why yes, I'm a man of God, dear brother," and the deal is then perfectly legitimate. The trick is getting God into the transaction and it's O.K. And some of those shepherds I've seen!

Havelock Ellis was not only the scientist and savant but a wonderful observer of general, everyday life and people. Looking back on that single evening I was with him and could listen with such pleasure to his gentle talk—for he had a most agreeable way of expressing himself—I think the strongest impression he made was one of serene lucidity. In him was nothing austere or remote and there was a great nobility about the handsome, ascetic head on the tall, lean body. In his way of listening there was ease and graciousness; in all there was a sort of richness of "peace" about him; such, I thought, was the aura. One felt that nothing, no matter how small, would bore him, providing it was authentic; and then one reflected that a fool and a knave are also of point for study. He was all-encompassing, and so keenly observant. And it is no doubt this, in part, which has given his book on Spain the reputation of being one of the best ever written on that country.

After that evening in 1926 my contacts with him were only two, and by correspondence, and both times it was about Spain. His reply to my "Enquête" addressed to the writers of Britain concerning their feeling about the Spanish war, published in 1937 as *Authors Take Sides*, is this: "While I recognize there are good men on both sides, I am myself decisively on the side of the legal Government and against Franco and Fascism."

A year later I wrote him from Barcelona telling him how Republican newspapers had published his voiced concern for the suffering endured by Spain, to which was now added dire hunger in the Republican zones. He answered me, pleased to learn that his sympathy had been recorded.

The Revaluation of Obscenity, which one might describe as a rich, objective essay or study of forty pages, was written before 1931, in fact in 1930. That is over twenty years before several cases of homosexuality were so publicly vented and commented upon by all sections of the press and public as well as in the Courts in England. Nowadays the stigma on the fact—and even on its discussion—is infinitely less than in the days of Wilde. Havelock Ellis was already writing in 1930 that the new attitude towards sex made it possible to evaluate sex questions more rationally than heretofore, and that this in itself suggested there should be a reassessment of "obscenity"—a term left vague by the Law.

Among the many interesting things he wrote in this volume are the following questions and points:

> We have already gone far in a corresponding task: the revaluation of sex with which obscenity has so largely been associated or confused. By the "obscene" we may properly mean what is *off the scene* and not openly shown on the stage of life.

There are two main adjuncts in obscenity, which he terms "Sexual processes" and "Excremental processes." There is an interesting difference, for, as he says, "The taboo of the excremental obscene is only conventional and social, while that on the sexual obscene is regarded as also moral and religious." Swift, as a man of the Church, eschewed "even the faintest recognition of the sexually obscene," but could be said to delight in the excremental obscene.

Morals change and are in constant flux; the word "immorality" may have been brought in by the Puritans. A danger, indeed, lies in words! Lawrence's *Lady Chatterley's Lover*, recognized as a fine work in itself, was banned as obscene on account of the use of plain, old English words, "in place of the euphemisms commonly preferred in the 'good society' of his age"—words such as a child may write in the street "without endangering the structure of society." During the Shakespearian era words now termed gross were in common use. In Goldsmith's time, the fashion had changed and Hazlitt records in his *Conversations* what Northcote told him of the protests that came from the gallery at some coarse word in a Goldsmith play. It was the common people, he said, who "sought for refinement as a treat; people in high life were fond of grossness and ribaldry as a relief to their overstrained affectation of gentility." And Havelock Ellis adds: "It is the populace that tend to enforce the tone in these matters and even to mould the law."

No agreement was there last century, he points out, as to any proper definition of obscenity in terms of law. It "usually meant at least two things . . . verbal nakedness or physical nakedness—the unclothing of something that in public is habitually clothed. But it also meant something sexually provocative. That was evidently essential. For unless this unclothing induced sexual activity how could it be 'immoral'; why should it be prohibited?" Fear of obscenity haunted the nineteenth century and "because science necessarily speaks without disguise" books of science were prosecuted and condemned. Among other books have been the Bible and works by Rabelais, Shakespeare, and Joyce.

"That which excites or promotes sexual desires" has

been one definition of obscenity in the law courts. By that score, says Havelock Ellis, if this be reasoned out it will be found that so many are the things that act as erotic fetiches (to conscious and subconscious minds alike) that even both sexes will have to go if "obscenity" is to be abolished! Discussion of birth control and combating of venereal disease have been retarded by the taboos on them.

Finally, that which is "off the scene" has nothing to do with pornography, and the case for this is admirably put.

A revaluation of obscenity is very far from meaning a justification of the things that most reasonable people find ugly and unpleasant. But it means a different attitude towards their suppression in practice. We know the results of the attitude which has prevailed in the past. We have all been victims of it. A premium is put on things that are dirty and worthless. It is law alone which makes pornography both attractive and profitable . . . As long as there is secrecy there will be pornography. Obscenity there will be under all systems, for it has a legitimate and natural foundation; but the vulgar, disgusting and stupid form of obscenity called pornography—the literature and art that is a substitute for the brothel and of the same coarse texture— has its foundation not on Nature but on artificial secrecy . . . *The Market in pornography is artificially created.* That is the central fact of the situation. No one would read a book because the Home Secretary recommends it; there is a vast public to read it because he condemns it.

Ellis's volume is bound in blue cloth boards. The spine of blue leather affords an attractive background for the gold letters of the title. Presumably owing to the great name of the author and the interest the public had in the subject, all the edition sold out. It was distributed in London, and I was never sent any of the reviews.

George Moore

The Talking Pine

The Talking Pine, a small fantasy by George Moore, was
merely a two-page *plaquette* in light beige paper covers.
It was never put on the market because George Moore
thought it too slight, after all, to be signed by him. And
yet he had agreed to let me print and publish this dream of
his, which he had had just before the last time, or one of
the very last times, I saw him, on December 9, 1930. He
was then eighty, and he told it to me so charmingly in his
"breakfast room" in Ebury Street that I seemed to see it
immediately in print. Maybe to appreciate it fully it needs
the slow, rolling rhythm of his voice. But it struck me that
day like a small piece of folklore connected with ancient
seas and man's agelong business with ships, and trade,
and travel, all spoken in the simplest terms, and yet
mysterious. Here it is.

A few nights ago I dreamt a poem in my armchair after dinner.
In it a man walked in a pine-forest admiring the trees that were
about him but not one fulfilled his ambition, which was to find the
tallest pine-tree in the world. In his wanderings he heard a voice,
and as nobody was about he concluded that it came from the
branches, but they were empty. At last the voice spoke to him out of
the earth, saying:

"I was once the tree that thou art in search of."

"And where art thou now?" the man asked.

"My roots are here," the voice answered, "but myself
is the mast of a great ship."

Whereupon I awoke in a great fright, overturning the electric
lamp at my elbow, but holding fast to the last line of my poem:

"Some dream of pine-trees, and some of ships!"

G. M. had sent me this later in writing and I thought he
would sign the edition of five hundred, which would
have been put on sale at 10s a copy, not £2 2s which he
thought I intended to ask. It was beautifully set and printed
on fine paper, and certainly to collectors of his work this
was not an excessive price, his signature alone often having
fetched more. However, there was nothing to do but
respect his decision, and reflect that—after so various a
number of authors printed and published by me between
the end of 1928 and the spring of 1931—it was George
Moore who had been the first and was now, in this
peculiar sense, the last of them all in my venture with the
Hours Press.

Epilogue

The Hours Press came to an end in the spring of 1931, myself away from Paris at that time, and hard at work on what was to become my large *Negro Anthology*. I cannot be sure, even now, if my Hours came to a timely or untimely end. To a timely one, I expect, and yet . . . which means that it would have continued, I think, had I been able to pass it on for a while to the ideal partner, had such a person existed. But even if I had been able to hand it over to that mythical ideal partner, could I have gone back to printing when *Negro* was out some three years later? I doubt it. This work, due to the strange events in life that sometimes engulf one, was the principal reason for my closing the press down. Doing *Negro* was entirely absorbing and to have gone on running the press at the same time seemed out of the question. Research, travel, writing cannot go with printing and publishing. The press was not making any money at that time, and the contracted manager had introduced all the usual business ways, "overheads," and who knows what else, which ate up the profits. The first year the press had been prosperous, partly owing to my simple way of doing things and doing as many things as possible myself. Now expenses were heavy, inexplicably so. In short, the whole thing had got out of hand. Yes, to a timely end it came.

Taking stock of what had been the Hours was not difficult, for nearly all the editions had sold out in their own time and several of them entirely on publication. On return to France, after getting *Negro* to come (how lengthily) into being and seeing it through the press and then appear in London, I gave up the Rue Guenégaud. All that I kept, save a few books and one case of type, was the great Mathieu press, which I moved back to Réanville out of sentiment and a nebulous feeling that, although publishing was doubtless over, there might yet be some other kind of printing to be done in the unpredictable future. The second press, the Minerva, with all its furnishings and type, I sold to the rising French publisher, Guy Levis Mano, who, I am told, still has it in use all these years later.

Back in its first home, the old converted stable, the Mathieu did eventually prove useful. In a year or two the future that had seemed so unpredictable was no longer unpredictable. War would probably come. To my mind "the open switch-on of modern times in our part of Europe" occurred in Paris with the *putsch* there on February 16, 1934, the same month that *Negro* appeared. After that the precipitation of events increased mightily and everything was obviously mounting to a peak. After Abyssinia came Spain, and it was during that war that the Mathieu once again became invaluable. With the help of the Chilean poet Pablo Neruda, and later alone, I set up, using the only case of type I had from the Hours, six *plaquettes* of poetry that were sold for Spanish Republican relief in Paris. The proofs were made on the Mathieu; however the actual printing had to be done in town. The fifth one contained Auden's *Spain*, the sixth, poems by Nicolas Guillén, Brian Howard, and Randall Swingler. This was in 1937, at the same time as my "Enquête" went out to writers in Britain asking for their opinions on the Spanish war and which were published later that year as *Authors Take Sides.*

It was in the same year in Spain that I listened to an unforgettable appreciation of the Hours Press. While I was sitting one night on the Ramblas in Barcelona with the well-known Spanish poet, Manuel Altolaguirre, he suddenly turned to me and said, "You know, I have been a printer too. Your Hours Press books, especially the poetry volumes, were an inspiration to me and your style pleased me so much that I even copied it at times. Did you not know?" He went on to talk of his months in London years before when he had started printing with almost no money. How many had been the difficulties. Working on such a limited budget meant that when the type was set for printing it had to be transported a considerable distance to a press. Taxis were too dear, so it was in a hooded baby pram that he and his wife would wheel the composition across Hyde Park to the printery. Along their route good British citizens, emerging from wintry evening mists, could be heard saying how disgraceful it was to take a baby out so late. Altolaguirre was a bit of a *gitano*, that is, he was very inventive, but knowing him as I did, I could not doubt the veracity of this tale. I too had carried immensely heavy weights about at one time, for example when the *plaquettes* of poems in several languages in aid of Spain had to go to Paris for printing. We went on discussing various forms and styles. To both our minds, the simplest was the best: fair type and beautiful paper, great legibility and a sort of spareness in everything. We found we were, in fact, purists.

As those years went by other echoes would come to me in various countries of "the press you had, the lovely books you produced." My home was still Réanville, my occupation mainly free-lance journalism. And then came World War II. For a year, until late 1940, I travelled in South America, Mexico, and the Antilles, with half the world between me and home. When France collapsed, I tried furiously to return to England, but the difficulties at that time were many and my voyage home was slow. When I did return, Hitler and Vichy were supreme and reports from France said that Normandy, in a general way, had come to very good terms with collaboration. Of Réanville, *that* was the only news I wanted.

How much I thought then about the old days—Réanville in the dripping mist, outside the printery; Réanville in the scorch of July at the beginning of G. M.'s *Peronnik*; Réanville of all those night hours among the circulars and address books spread over the floor. I thought about the way of life in 1928—Aragon composing designs for *Snark* (where might he be now?)—Henry's wafted music, *Rhapsody in Blue* (in what country was he at present?). I thought constantly about the admirable couple in the village inn, Jean and Georgette Goasguën, so well, so happily known first of all during that dangerous year, 1939. How were they faring? I thought of my many Spanish friends in France, and wondered what was happening to them? To all this, and how much more, there was no reply. Then came the time when I heard of the brief personal messages that could be sent through the International Red Cross, and though answers could take up to three months, it was wonderful to be thus a little in touch again. By 1943, little twenty-five word messages came from Normandy every three to six months. They were in code, and I remember this one from Georgette. "Jean's health now better. Mayor wanted to send him to jail. Same illness as Carmen's father." What it meant was that Jean had been in danger, that the mayor had tried to send him to jail for political reasons. "Carmen's father," a Spanish republican, had been imprisoned by Franco in 1939. Although I knew this only later, the Goasguëns had, at the risk of their lives, removed all that they could from Le Puits Carré and had hidden it in the inn. They had defied the orders of the mayor, and had continued to rescue what was possible from the monumental pillage going on at my home. From Georgette came this message immediately after the liberation of Normandy: "*Plus rien*"—All's gone.

Somehow the words were no surprise, and the more I thought about it all, the less. That highly civilized country, France, had some very disagreeable things to it, but this state of war mentality might be as bad anywhere in the same circumstances? Well I remembered how those who thought and felt one way in the village lived, and acted, in daily detestation of those who felt otherwise. What could I have seemed to them, I, a foreign woman actually engaged at one time in *printing*. That this had been as long as ten years ago and more would make no difference. Printing! And printing what? A press is very dangerous! It means the dissemination of ideas, obviously very bad ones in this case—foreign, for a start. That would be the line taken in general at Réanville, I thought. And the account of two people who had escaped from the village just before the Germans arrived, although it made me angry, was not particularly surprising to me. Yes, the French police had come to the house. It was in March 1940, before Hitler was on the move, during the phoney-war period. They had made a thorough search, were particularly interested in books and papers. What was this press they had been informed of? It was shown them by the friend at that moment in charge of the house, but the look of it told them nothing. What had it printed? They ordered every Hours Press book to be given them and took them away; it seems they returned some of them later after inspection. At this date, England and France were allies. But "we feel sure you would have been arrested that day," said those who were describing it all with indignation. That the printery had been shut and no output had come from it for so many years meant nothing. The rumor must have gone round that it was printing clandestine sheets of something or other that were somehow "dangerous." At this point I thought wryly of the difficulties M. Lévy and I had had with slow speed and pressure, and many a single page. Clandestine sheets for mass distribution, *indeed*!

The Allied armies were now sweeping through my part of Normandy, and Vernon, the large local town near Réanville, suddenly came into the news, and big news it was too. Here the Americans and British were said to have made "some beautifully simple manoeuvre which fooled the enemy and drove them out in practically no time." It was then that my dear friend, Morris Gilbert, the well-known American journalist who was then on active service, came into the picture. And it is with heart-beat that I continue to salute him for what he contrived to do. He managed to make one leap to Réanville while at his work of printing sheets that were placed on village walls announcing the progress of the liberation. He had gone to Réanville to find the Goasguëns, and as he entered their inn they threw up their arms and exclaimed, "*Tu viens de la part de Nancy*," guessing that he could not have come but from me. The Germans had left just two hours before. There was no wine to drink, but there was some "mente et citron," and while they talked and drank a dogfight took place right over their heads. When it was over, Jean took Morris to Le Puits Carré to see the wreckage. In London, a few days later, I received Morris's superb description of what he had seen.

And there, amid the familiar sights of shambles and destruction, he had seen . . . yes, what? The collapse of everything save the roof. No doors, no windows, no furniture left. Books, books, books, flung higgle-piggle all over the bathroom floor, well stamped and walked on for years by now—a sort of mattress of books, thick and deep. When he came to London on leave that last autumn of the war it was with a copy of Norman Douglas's *One Day* in his hands. It had caught his eye, floating there, right on top. There was a strange smell of all the past to it. Did I mind his taking it? He had, in some sort, stolen it, had he not? We found the word inapplicable, as did Norman Douglas, with whom we had a commemorative drink. This copy of his signed red leather edition had stood up well to the ordeal. Had Morris Gilbert seen what had happened to the press? Yes . . . no . . . He had had only a few moments there in all this welter. The roof was off it anyway. So, for the next several months in London, a daily cog in the war machinery, I could now evoke some sort of visual picture of Réanville. The big old thyme bush, at least, would be left, I thought, but I later found it was not.

When I did get back to Réanville in March 1945 and sat in the "Coq Gaulois," the Goasguën's inn, Jean and Georgette wondered if I would not be overcome by the sight of my house. Even now I cannot analyze my strange feeling. It was "a discovery of something entirely new, bound up with something entirely past." In a dream I wandered alone through the shell of my home. And it was, at first, with the sense of touching the possessions of another that I said: "Let me be practical! Let me see—and save—what is left, for the pillage is still going on." By then the Goasguëns had yet more of my things: books, papers, articles, photographs, on top of what they had already carried away at night for safekeeping before the German troops were billeted in the house.

Five years of destruction had gone on, but by now the bathroom floor had been cleared of its "mattress." Georgette had understood my telegraphed request from London: "I beg you, take the shovel to it all!" Out of that litter emerged, gradually, many an item connected with the Hours.

What was this in the bath torn away from its fittings? The two stone heads from Easter Island that Alvaro Guevara had given me years after I had printed *St. George,* one of them broken in two (that must have taken some doing). And this, nailed firmly to a window in lieu of glass? The once green vellum covers of Rodker's large and beautiful edition of Ezra Pound's *Cantos*; its companion, the Three Mountains Press edition of the earlier *Cantos,* had disappeared. Sticking out of some debris was my father's first letter, torn out of a family album, dated in the early 1850's when father was around four. I read, "I am a good boy. I know my letters." On the mantelpiece in the same ravaged bedroom stood a large question mark in red and black cardboard—*that* had never been mine. Here, flung face down and horribly creased, was my lovely blue landscape by Tanguy, so much in the spirit of the "cliff-scapes" he had made for Lowenfels's *Apollinaire.* It was shot full of bullet holes, ten small, one large. Most of the other paintings and drawings had disappeared, although there was still half an abstract, torn roughly across, by the surrealist artist, Malkine, whom I had liked so much. And I saw what looked like a bayonet thrust through a part of the portrait Eugene MacCown had done of me in Paris in 1923. Of the large, very rare 1598 edition of "The Workes of our Antient and Lerned English Poet, Geffrey Chavcer" remained the covers, frontispiece, and a few pages. The valuable oriental rugs had all gone and the Hispano-Moorish chest that had contained the African beadings that used to deck the Rue Guenégaud was no more, save for a few of its drawers. Traces of beads were left, mere fragments in the passage under the straw that all soldiers seem to leave behind them, and a fury of hatred must have gone into pounding them to pieces. Of the entire collection of African and other primitive sculpture not one single piece remained, and most of the African ivory bracelets had vanished along with the trunk they were in. Georgette had picked up some of them in the fields, mostly those thin, disclike ones that Man Ray had photographed for *Henry-Music*. Everything that had survived, save a few remnants by assiduousness brought back to light, was thanks to that admirable pair of true friends. They would leave, they said. The spirit in the village was infamous; I too would see that no return there was possible, no!

Among the first questions asked of me was, "What was your press for?" It would have been useless to point out that an ancient hand press that had been out of use for years would be quite incapable of turning out anything like a newspaper; I was printing "secret newspapers" it had been said! *Who* was there to manufacture them? I asked, and there was no reply. The house had been empty, quite empty a very long time. And then, thanks to the village mayor (who had also tried to sell it during the

course of the war, saying everything now belonged to
the Germans) it had been occupied by the German troops
he had encouraged to go there. Pillage before, pillage then,
and pillage after they left. That covered the turbid, brutal,
horrible story.

Many people came to the "Coq Gaulois" to denounce
each other to me and to tell me what had happened, but
only the so-called village idiot, Jean Marie, seemed worth
listening to at that moment, so droll was he, a drunk,
whom I made drunker yet so as to hear more. Meanwhile
the mayor had been asked, even ordered, to return all my
keys to me. There seemed no point in interrupting the
unsavory if interesting flow of denunciations. How funny
it was for me, the child of a very conservative British
father who had remained mid-Victorian in many severe
ways, to hear that the German troops had been ordered
to collect all the ancient volumes of that famous English
weekly, *Punch*. Whoever it was that gave that order may
have looked inside a number on the Franco-German war,
say in 1870, and seeing caricatures of German officers
shouted: "*Dass auch muss gehen.*" So the sixty or so volumes
of *Punch*, dating from about 1832 to 1882, were ceremoni-
ously burned on the grass in front of the house. After this,
the German troops broke and burned everything not of
immediate use to them. I learned that they had put the
African sculpture up on the wall near the house, stoned it,
and then destroyed it completely. They had even hacked
to pieces the massive old beam which had been the main
one of the printery, along with all the rest of the wood-
work there. The roof had been torn off too. To the venerable iron Mathieu Press, still standing there, it seems they
did nothing, no doubt because its size made it impossible
to move. It remained solid and seemingly intact if very

rusty. The only piece of furniture left in the house was a massive old oak table, on which I now write this. Then after the Germans departed came the lovers and defecators, to enjoy the privacy of this half-open, half-enclosed ruin. Outside under a tree, all mashed and earth-trodden, I found a drawing by Wyndham Lewis. The lindens nearby, beneath which Norman Douglas, Frank Hutchinson, and I had sat in 1938, had grown strangely tall. The one thing I felt sure of seeing again was the peculiar old round thyme bush, in the ragged back part of the garden. But no matter how often I thought of it, I finally had to admit that it had vanished. The missing bush seemed to say: "No more, no more of any of this for you. Don't try to come back." The outhouse, which had stored many books in those printing years, still bore the sign scratched in rough chalk: "*Achtung! Waffen!*"—Arms and munitions in here! Down the deep well, I was told, had been thrown a small sheep to putrify, books, excrement, an old chintz cover from the sofa, and two rifles. All by now I thought would be compost.

It was no sense of fatalism that made me accept the sack and loot, the ruin and end of Le Puits Carré. The very word "accept" is wrong, for one is not in a position to "accept" or to "refuse" a fact. Do either and nothing will be any different. No bombs, no artillery, no air raids, no shooting war had there been just here at any time, but a detestable, permanent war-within-war of hatred in the village. That is what I realized as the spate of almost incomprehensible narration rolled for days over my head. An absence of five years and more now led to . . . to what? To a sort of voyage of discovery—of the *discovery of destruction*, and within it there was an element of "return after death."

One day three little children helped me rake the straw left in the house. They said the German troops had been there for about three months. Someone else remembered "they had arrived at the time of the wedding." Whose? No one could, or would, remember anything like even the most approximate date. All was in a daze.

Three long days went by raking through fragments in the stillness and peculiar odor of the gutted house. It was maybe last of all that some thirty letters of Caslon type came to light. They were in an old tin cigarette box, one of six that some frantic individual (drunk maybe?) had so evidently tried to hammer to pieces. This, passingly, seemed a symbolic exclamation: "Damnation take all print!" And how well illustrated here was that famous cry: "Death to the intellect!" which was shouted in Germany and then in Spain.

It seemed as if, overnight, a few more papers and fragments had floated down onto the diminishing litter, for here, today and surely not yesterday, was suddenly that photograph of Ezra Pound's premature deathmask, and some of the press circulars and other finds of that kind. But not *one* of the mass of letters to do with the Hours remained, not one save two or three from George Moore. All the hundreds that had accrued throughout the years from writers and artists, from friends and enemies, were gone—gone forever into the domain of what one now called "Before." Gone were those of Arthur Symons, Aldous Huxley, Michael Arlen, Richard Aldington, Ezra Pound, T. S. Eliot, Wyndham Lewis, Robert Graves, Robert Nichols, Ronald Firbank, Roy Cambell, Osbert Sitwell, T.W. Earp, St. John Hutchinson, Iris Tree, Evan Morgan, Clifford Sharp, founder and editor of the *New Statesman and Nation*, Raymond Mortimer, Geoffrey

Scott, John Strachey, Alvaro Guevara, and of how many, many more. Gone too were the "literary" letters of such French writers as Aragon, Breton, Tzara, Creval, and others. Gone were at least three-quarters of the material I used in *Negro*, several hundred volumes of articles, photographs, and documents on color. And most of the articles, books, poems, translations, and letters of the Spanish war years were also missing. How well, without benefit of bombs, may all the stuff of forty years be ravaged in a few days.

Enough remained, however, to show what had been there, enough, alas, to create a housing problem for the next several years. At the end of the collecting, what I had salvaged, books apart, came to fifteen large cases and sacks of papers. I had been through every single inch of debris, and I had to agree with Georgette's exclamation that I was indeed *une vraie pillouillere*, a born scavenger. But if much was left, far more was gone forever, which seems to me the answer to the question one asks as a child: "What is Life going to be like?" A big question, it gets a big answer.

Conditions at Réanville showed it would be impossible to live there again. Still baffled by what I felt at meeting all this, I seemed to sense a slowly hardening core of anger growing within me. Yes, it was the fate of the books and works of art that had profoundly shocked and infuriated me. Irreplaceable books, documents, paintings, letters— all *finis*. So much was gone forever.

It was just after this first visit to what had been the home of the Hours that I went to the British Embassy in Paris at the invitation of Sir Alfred and Lady Diana Duff Cooper, friends of a lifetime. The end of the war was now in sight, but how long would it take for anything to become normal again? Many years, obviously, and much would never be the same. Where was I going to live now, and how? Friends were dispersed, my best one possibly dead. The cost of living was appalling; repairs and restorations and taking things up again—so many dreams. Pretty soon, too, all the remains of Le Puits Carré would have to be stored, for the Goasguëns were anxious to leave at once.

No such thoughts were in mind during the pleasant hour or more in the Embassy. Among the few guests was Stuart Gilbert, the expert on James Joyce, whom I had met many years before when my press was still working. He was very courteous and cordial with me and we talked of the war and of return to France, and of how it felt now, and things like that. It seems to me we had no conversation at all about the old days, about "Before."

And then something he said made me start, and I, who had never actually seen it, seemed now to gaze upon "that mattress of books on the bathroom floor," and all it represented. At one go, the past surged up over me in one huge wave. And yet his voice had been as soft and remote as one imagines that of an oracle to be. But the roles were reversed, as if the oracle were questioning, the oracle making enquiry of the questioner, for what should come from his lips, so gently said, but, "Are you going to start the Hours Press again?"

Bibliography of Hours Press Publications

1928

Aldington, Richard. *Hark the Herald.* December. 5½ by 7½. 2 pp. 100 hand-set, signed copies, Vergé de Rives, 17 pt. Caslon Old Face. Mary blue wrappers. Title in gold letters on front wrapper. A present to the author; not for sale.

Douglas, Norman. *Report on the Pumice-Stone Industry of the Lipari Islands.* June. 6 by 10. 6 pp. 80 hand-set copies; ordinary commercial paper. 11 pt. Caslon Old Face. Title printed on front. A present to the author; not for sale.

Moore, George. *Peronnik the Fool.* December. 6 by 9. 63 pp. 200 hand-set, signed copies; Vergé de Rives, 11 pt. Caslon Old Face. Title stamped in gold on front, pale blue board covers. £2.

1929

Aldington, Richard. *The Eaten Heart.* Late winter. 7 by 11. 28 pp. 200 hand-set, signed copies, Canson-Montgolfier. 16 pt. Caslon Old Face. Title on front, gilt lettering on green marble paper. £1 1s.

Aragon, Louis. *La Chasse au Snark.* Early winter. 9 by 12. 30 pp. 300 hand-set, signed copies, Alfa paper. 16 pt. Caslon Old Face. Title on front designed and composed by Aragon, in typographical patterns and letterings on dull scarlet paper boards. Also 5 copies, Japan paper; same size, binding. 300 copies at £1 1s. Japan paper copies at £5 5s.

Douglas, Norman. *One Day.* July. 6 by 10. 55 pp. 200 signed copies, Velin de Rives, Monotype. Title stamped in gilt scarlet leather. £3 3s. Also 300 copies; same size, type, Vergé de Vidalon, puce colored boards. £1 10s.

Bibliography of Publications

Guevara, Alvaro. *St George at Silene.* January. 10 by 13. 4 pp. 150 hand-set, signed copies, Velin de Rives. 16 pt. Caslon Old Face. Title, front and back, endpapers, designed by author. Grey paper, stitched covers. 10s 6d.

Symons, Arthur. *Mes Souvenirs.* July. 6 by 10. 48 pp. 200 signed copies, Velin de Rives. Bound beige cloth boards. £2 2s.

1930

Beckett, Samuel. *Whoroscope.* Midsummer. 6 by 9. 6 pp. 100 signed, hand-set copies, and 200 unsigned copies. Both on Vergé de Rives. 11 pt. Caslon Old Face. Title in black ink on dark red paper; upper cover, white band affixed, stating that poem had won the Hours Press £10 prize for the best poem on "Time." Signed copies: 5s; unsigned: 1s.

Campbell, Roy. *Poems.* July. 7 by 11. 24 pp. 200 hand-set, signed copies, Canson-Montgolfier. 16 pt. Caslon Old Face. Title lettered in gilt on leather spine; Vermilion paper boards, with two drawings by Campbell. £1 10s.

Crowder, Henry. *Henry-Music.* December. 10 by 13. 20 pp. 150 copies, signed by composer. Hard board covers, front and back different, specially designed photomontages by Man Ray. 10s 6d

Graves, Robert. *Ten Poems More.* Early spring. 7 by 11. 24 pp. 200 signed, hand-set copies, Canson-Montgolfier. 16 pt. Caslon Old Face. Title stamped on dark leather spine. Covers, both different, photomontages by Len Lye. £1 10s.

Lowenfels, Walter. *Apollinaire.* Early. 7 by 11. 16 pp. 150 signed, hand-set copies, Canson-Montgolfier. 16 pt. Caslon Old Face. Title, stamped gilt on leather spine. Covers, both different, specially designed by Yves Tanguy, printed black on daffodil colored paper boards. £1 10s.

MacCown, Eugene. *Catalogue of Paintings, Drawings and Gouaches by Eugene MacCown.* Early. 6 by 10. 20 pp. 1000 copies, Caslon Old Face Italics, Vergé de Rives. A present to the artist; not for sale.

Bibliography of Publications

Pound, Ezra. *A Draft of XXX Cantos.* Midsummer. 5 by 8. 142 pp. 200 copies and 10 signed copies (with two copies on real vellum for the author). The 200 copies pn Canson-Montgolfier-Soleil Velin. The 10 signed copies on Texas Mountain paper; 200 copies in stout beige linen boards; title stamped in red on spine and upper cover. 10 copies in vermilion leather, with same lettering. Both with initial letters at start of each Canto by the poet's wife, Dorothy Shakespear. Ten copies at £5 5s. 200 copies at £2.

Riding, Laura. *Twenty Poems Less.* Spring. 7 by 11. 40 pp. 200 signed, hand-set copies, Canson-Montgolfier. 16 pt. Caslon Old Face. Title stamped gilt on dark leather spine. Covers, both different, photomontages by Len Lye. £1 10s.

——. *Four Unposted Letters to Catherine.* Early summer. 6 by 8. 50 pp. 200 signed copies, Haut Vidalon, Garamond Italic. Title gilt lettered on dark leather spine. Covers, both different, designed photomontages by Len Lye. £2.

Rodker, John. *Collected Poems.* August. 6 by 10. 36 pp. 200 signed copies, hand-made paper, initial lettering by Edward Wadsworth. Title lettered in gilt on dark leather spine. Covers, both different, specially designed montages by Len Lye. £1 10s.

1931

Acton, Harold. *This Chaos.* January. 7 by 11. 32 pp. 150 hand-set, signed copies, Canson-Montgolfier. 16 pt. Caslon Old Face. Paper boards, title lettered in gilt on leather spine. Covers, both different, specially designed abstracts, printed blue, by Elliott Seabrooke. £1 10s.

Aldington, Richard. *Last Straws.* January. 6 by 10. 61 pp. 200 signed copies in green suede cloth boards; title lettered in gilt on upper cover; and 300 additional copies in grey-brown paper boards, design by Douglas Cockerell, with printed label on upper cover. Signed copies at £2; unsigned copies at 7s 6d.

Brown, Bob. *Words.* January. 7 by 11. 23 pp. 150 signed, hand-set copies, Canson-Montgolfier. 16 pt. Caslon Old Face. Title lettered in gilt on leather spine. Upper cover designed in letterings by John Sibthorpe. £1 10s.

Bibliography of Publications

Ellis, Havelock. *The Revaluation of Obscenity*. Spring. 6 by 10. 40 pp. 200 signed copies. Type and paper unknown to Miss Cunard. Blue leather spine on blue cloth boards. £2.

Howard, Brian. *First Poems*. January. 7 by 11. 48 pp. 150 signed, handset copies, Canson-Montgolfier. 16 pt. Caslon Old Face. Title lettered in gilt on dark leather spine. Pale blue paper boards; special designs, upper and lower covers different, by John Banting. £1 10s.

Moore, George. *The Talking Pine*. Early. 8 by 10. A 2-leaf plaquette, 500 copies. Light beige paper covers. Paper and type unknown to Miss Cunard. Not for sale.

Index

Acton, Harold: visits Hours Press, 86, 164–65; and Brian Howard, 161–62; career of, 161, 162, 163; *This Chaos*, 161, 167–68; contributes to *Grand Man*, 163; friendship with Douglas, 163, 164

Aldington, Richard: requests printing of *Hark the Herald*, 39; *Eaten Heart*, 51, 54, 57; assists James Hanley, 52–53; career of, 52–54, 156, 157; suggests Hours Press poetry contest, 109; meets Beckett, 112; *Last Straws*, 158–59; reviews of *Last Straws*, 159; dispute over royalties, 160

Altolaguirre, Manuel: discusses printing with Nancy Cunard, 197

Antheil, George, 178

Apollinaire, Guillaume, 96

Aragon, Louis: at Réanville, 8, 9–10, 11, 12, 13–14; and surrealism, 42, 43, 79, 80; translates *Snark*, 43–44, 48–50; prints *Snark*, 45–46, 47; character of, 46–47; prints "Voyageur," 48; estimate of Lowenfels, 94

Arlen, Michael, xi, 31

Banting, John: designs covers for *First Poems*, 81, 175

Beckett, Samuel: description of, 111–12, 117; writes *Whoroscope*, 111, 117–18; assists Joyce, 112, 115; text of *Whoroscope*, 118–22; text of "From the only Poet to a Shining Whore," 155

Beecham, Thomas, Sir, 116, 117

Bell, Clive: contributes to MacCown catalogue, 88

Bird, William: sells Three Mountains press to Nancy Cunard, xii, 4, 6

Boyle, Kay, 178

Breton, André: and surrealism, 79, 80; his studio, 164; mentioned, 42, 43

Breton, Susan: visits Hours Press, 46

Brown, Robert C.: *Words*, 81, 177, 181, 182–85; character and career of, 177–81; *1450–1950*, 177, 178; *Gems: A Censored Anthology*, 179–80; Reading Machine, 179, 181–83; Roving Eye Press, 180, 181; *Readies*, 181; excerpts from *Gems*, 188–89

Bunting, Basil: reviews Pound's *Cantos*, 130–31

Campbell, Roy: makes designs for *Poems*, 81; description of, 133–34, 137; and Spanish Civil War, 137–38; *Poems*, 139, 140; text of "The Olive Tree," 139–40; review of "Tree," 139

Carroll, Lewis: *Snark* translated by Aragon, 43, 44, 48–49

Chattopadhya, Sarojini: "Magic of the East," 72

Cocteau, Jean: contributes to MacCown catalogue, 88; mentioned, 87

Crevel, René: and surrealism, 42; mentioned, 87

Crosby, Harry and Caresse, 178

Crowder, Henry: composes music for *Henry-Music*, xvi, 147, 148, 149, 150; meets Nancy Cunard, 26, 29; joins Hours Press, 26, 29; talks with Aldington, 53, 156; crashes car, 54; and Lowenfels, 93; description of, 148–49; *Henry-Music*, 150, 151, 152, 155, 203; and Samuel Beckett, 155; mentioned, 51, 64, 81, 137

Cunard, Bache, Sir, viii

Index

Cunard, Maud (Emerald), Lady, viii–ix, 116, 117, 123
Cunard, Nancy: childhood of, viii–x; resides in Paris, xi; compiles *Negro*, xii, 26, 84, 94, 118, 152, 186, 195, 207; interest in surrealism, xiv, 76, 79–80, 84; involvement in Spanish Civil War, xiv, xvii, 189–90, 196, 197; on printing, 7, 10, 11, 12, 19, 20–21; ethnographical interests, 80, 82; meets Samuel Beckett, 111–12; meets James Joyce, 115–17; circulates Scottsboro appeal, 128–29; writes "Equatorial Way" and "Blues," 149, 150, 152; on Negro culture, 152; prints Spanish war poetry, 196; edits *Authors Take Sides*, 197; returns to Réanville (1945), 201. *See also* Hours Press
Cunard, Victor, 59

Douglas, Norman: sends *Lipari Islands* to Hours Press, xii–xiii, 10–12; issues private editions, 23, 60–61; *One Day*, 23, 60, 62, 64–65, 201; description of, 59–61; visits Hours Press, 86; sketched by MacCown, 87; friendship with Lowenfels, 92–93; and Acton, 163, 164; mentioned, 15, 65, 201
Duchamp, Marcel, 81

Earp, T. W.: comments on Campbell, 133, 134
Eliot, T. S.: *Ara Vus Prec*, 142
Ellis, Havelock: importance of, 186–90; Brown's comments on, 188–89; reply to *Authors Take Sides*, 189; *Revaluation of Obscenity*, 190–92; mentioned, 72
Eluard, Paul: and surrealism, 42, 43, 79

Faÿ, Bernard: contributes to MacCown catalogue, 88; mentioned, 87
Fitts, Dudley: reviews Pound's *Cantos*, 130, 131
Flanner, Janet: quoted, 6

Garvey, Marcus: movement of, 149–50
Gide, André: contributes to MacCown catalogue, 88
Gilbert, Morris: visits Réanville, 200–201
Gilbert, Stuart, 208
Goasguën, Jean and Georgette: messages to Nancy Cunard from, 198–99; welcome Nancy Cunard, 201; save Hours Press material, 202, 203, 207; mentioned, 198, 200, 208
Graves, Robert: success of *Ten Poems More*, 97; Seizin Press, 97, 106; description of, 98; text of "Oak, Poplar, Pine" and "Act V, Scene V," 99–100; *Ten Poems More* reviewed, 100, 103
Guevara, Alvaro: character of, 31–34; *St. George at Silene*, 34, 37–38, 39; Pound comments on, 34, 37

Hamnett, Nina: describes Campbell, 138
Hemingway, Ernest: discusses Pound, 127–28
Hours Press: founding of, xii, 3–16 *passim*; publications of, xii–xv, 15; sponsors poetry contest, xvi, 109–11; destruction of (Réanville), xviii, 98, 199–208 *passim*; objectives, 7; royalties paid by, 14; publicity, 14; distribution of books, 14–15; prices, 65; moves to Paris, 74–75; profits of, 74, 195; Paris location of, 76, 83, 84, 86; Paris series of Hours Press books, 80–82, 98; reviews of Hours Press books, 82–83; refuge for French student, 83–84; investigated, 84–86; managed by Mrs. Henderson, 147; issues Hours Press booklet, 147; closing of, 195–96
Howard, Brian: career and character of, 169–73; *First Poems*, 169, 171, 173–75; friendship with Acton, 171; *First Poems* reviewed, 175–76

John, Augustus, 32, 71, 137
Joyce, James: visits Nancy Cunard, 115–17; receives Pound's assistance, 123

214

Lawrence, D. H., 53
Lévy, Maurice: at Réanville, 9–10, 11,
  18, 19–21, 22, 23, 38, 39; character of,
  12–14; and *Snark*, 45–46, 47; leaves
  Hours Press, 76; mentioned, 6, 51, 64,
  200
Lewis, Wyndham: receives Pound's
  assistance, 123; paints Pound, 124
Lowenfels, Lillian, 53, 93
Lowenfels, Walter: *Apollinaire*, 81, 86,
  95–96, 181, 202; friendship with
  Douglas, 86, 92–93; career and char-
  acter of, 92–95; *Finale of Seem*, 93–94;
  wins Aldington prize, 94; *Sonnets of
  Love and Liberty*, 94; association with
  Brown, 181
Lye, Len: designs covers for Hours Press
  books, 81, 97, 104, 108, 143

McAlmon, Robert, 4–5
MacCown, Eugene: description of, 87;
  paints portrait of Nancy Cunard, 87,
  203; *Paintings, Drawings and Gouaches*,
  87–91
Mano, Guy Levis: buys Hours Press
  equipment, 196
Masson, André: visits Hours Press, 46
Mavrogordato, John: visits Hours Press,
  38
Moffet, Curtis: interests Nancy Cunard
  in African art, 80
Moore, George: visits Nevill Holt, ix;
  advises Nancy Cunard, x; submits
  Peronnik to Hours Press, xiii, 17–18;
  last visit with Nancy Cunard, xv, 193;
  Peronnik, 17–22, 24–26, 30, 82; *The
  Talking Pine*, 193–94
Mortimer, Raymond: contributes to
  MacCown catalogue, 91

Negro: published, 196. *See also* Cunard,
  Nancy

Orioli, Pino: publishes Lungarno Editions, 60, 61; mentioned, 23

Patmore, Bridget, 53
Pound, Dorothy: draws initials for
  Cantos, 131; mentioned, 52
Pound, Ezra: confers with Lady Cunard,
  123; description of, 123–24, 127; and
  fascism, 127–28; supports Scottsboro
  case, 128–29; anti-Semitism of, 129; *A
  Draft of XXX Cantos*, 129, 131, 202;
  comments on *Cantos*, 130; reviews of
  Cantos, 130–31; mentioned, 52, 53
Presses, private: described, vii–viii; Three
  Mountains, xii, 4–5, 129; importance
  of, xv–xvii; Contact Editions, 4–5;
  Hogarth, 5; Beaumont, 5; Ovid, 5,
  129; Nonesuch, 5; Fanfrolico, 5; Seizin,
  5, 97, 106; Black Sun, 6, 177; Black
  Manikin, 6; Aquila, 168

Ray, Man: creates covers for *Henry-
  Music*, 81, 151; estimate of, 151; mentioned, 79
Riding, Laura: and Seizin Press, 97, 106;
  Twenty Poems Less, 103; effect of
  poetry on Nancy Cunard, 103–4;
  description of, 104–5, 106; "Egypt,"
  105; influenced by Gertrude Stein,
  106; *Four Unposted Letters to Catherine*,
  106, 108; reviews of, 107; Aldington
  comments on, 108
Rodker, John: description of, 141–42;
  starts Casanova Society and Ovid
  Press, 142; *Collected Poems*, 143;
  author's introduction to *Collected
  Poems*, 143–44; text of "Hymn of
  Hymns," 144–46
Rothchild, Herbert L., 132

Sadoul, Georges: works at Hours Press,
  75–76; and surrealism, 80
Seabrooke, Elliott: designs covers of *This
  Chaos*, 81, 168
Sibthorpe, John: designs covers of *Words*,
  81, 182–83; joins Hours Press, 147
Sitwell, Edith: portrait of, 33
Surrealism: discussed, 40, 76, 79–80. *See
  also*, Cunard, Nancy.

Index

Symons, Arthur: interest in Hours Press, 66; writing discussed, 66–67, 72–73; meets Verlaine, 67–70; *Mes Souvenirs*, 67; "Verlaine," 69–71; "Bohemian Chelsea," 71–72; confides in Sarojini Chattopadhya, 72; friendship with Havelock Ellis, 186

Tanguy, Yves: designs covers of *Apollinaire*, 81, 96; mentioned, 76, 79, 202

Theis, Louise, 53
Thirion, André: helps Hours Press, 75; mentioned, 84
Tree, Iris: unpublished poems of, 82; mentioned, 32, 72

Wilde, Oscar: meets Arthur Symons, 71
Woolf, Leonard and Virginia: quoted, 8

Zadkine, Ossip: advises Lowenfels, 93